Cambridge Elei

Elements in Language Tez
edited by
Heath Rose
Linacre College, University of Oxford
Jim McKinley
University College London

PEDAGOGICAL TRANSLANGUAGING

Jasone Cenoz
University of the Basque Country

Durk Gorter
*University of the Basque Country and
Ikerbasque*

CAMBRIDGE
UNIVERSITY PRESS

CAMBRIDGE
UNIVERSITY PRESS

University Printing House, Cambridge CB2 8BS, United Kingdom

One Liberty Plaza, 20th Floor, New York, NY 10006, USA

477 Williamstown Road, Port Melbourne, VIC 3207, Australia

314–321, 3rd Floor, Plot 3, Splendor Forum, Jasola District Centre,
New Delhi – 110025, India

103 Penang Road, #05–06/07, Visioncrest Commercial, Singapore 238467

Cambridge University Press is part of the University of Cambridge.

It furthers the University's mission by disseminating knowledge in the pursuit of
education, learning, and research at the highest international levels of excellence.

www.cambridge.org
Information on this title: www.cambridge.org/9781009014403
DOI: 10.1017/9781009029384

First published 2021

A catalogue record for this publication is available from the British Library.

ISBN 978-1-009-01440-3 Paperback
ISSN 2632-4415 (online)
ISSN 2632-4407 (print)

Pedagogical Translanguaging

Elements in Language Teaching

DOI: 10.1017/9781009029384
First published online: December 2021

Jasone Cenoz
University of the Basque Country

Durk Gorter
University of the Basque Country and Ikerbasque

Author for correspondence: Jasone Cenoz, jasone.cenoz@ehu.eus

Abstract: Learning through the medium of a second or additional language is becoming very common in different parts of the world because of the increasing use of English as the language of instruction and because of the mobility of populations. This situation demands a specific approach that considers multilingualism as its core. Pedagogical translanguaging is a theoretical and instructional approach that aims at improving language and content competences in school contexts by using resources from the learner's whole linguistic repertoire. Pedagogical translanguaging is learner centred and endorses the support and development of all the languages used by learners. It fosters the development of metalinguistic awareness by softening boundaries between languages when learning languages and content. This Element looks at the way pedagogical translanguaging can be applied in language and content classes and how it can be valuable for the protection and promotion of minority languages. This title is also available as Open Access on Cambridge Core.

This Element also has a video abstract:
www.cambridge.org/pedagogical-translanguaging

Keywords: CLIL, metalinguistic awareness, minority languages, multilingual education, translanguaging

ISBNs: 9781009014403 (PB), 9781009029384 (OC)
ISSNs: 2632-4415 (online), 2632-4407 (print)

Contents

1 Introduction

Learning through the medium of a second or additional language is becoming very common in different parts of the world because of the increasing use of English as the language of instruction and because of the mobility of populations. These changes result in a situation that demands a specific approach that considers multilingualism as its core. *Pedagogical translanguaging* is a theoretical and instructional approach that aims at improving language and content competences in school contexts by using resources from the learner's whole linguistic repertoire. Pedagogical translanguaging is about activating multilingual speakers' resources so as to expand language and content learning. Multilinguals have broader repertoires than monolinguals, and they are often more experienced language learners. However, the potential of multilingual students based on their repertoire has not been fully developed because traditionally schools have adopted monolingual ideologies and have isolated languages in the curriculum. This is even the case when schools work towards the development of multilingual competences.

The aim of this Element is to provide the framework for pedagogical translanguaging, which proposes planned activities involving two or more languages so that languages reinforce one another and multilingual students make the most of their linguistic repertoire and their experience as language learners and language users. Pedagogical translanguaging is closely related to the original approach to translanguaging in Welsh bilingual education but goes beyond both the theory and practice of language alternation. Pedagogical translanguaging is learner centred and endorses the support and development of all the languages used by learners. It fosters the development of metalinguistic awareness by softening boundaries between languages when learning languages and content. In this Element, the characteristics of pedagogical translanguaging are explained as compared with other multilingual approaches used in educational contexts. This Element also looks at the way pedagogical translanguaging can be applied in language and content classes, and how it can be valuable for the protection and promotion of minority languages.

Pedagogical translanguaging goes against the strong language separation ideologies that are well rooted at schools and are based on two ideas. The first is that students can get confused if they are exposed to more than one language at a time and that the ideal situation occurs when the school organisation reinforces separation by having different teachers for each language and a strict differentiation in the allocation of spaces and times for each language. Inside the classroom, the principle is that only the target language is used, thus avoiding the use of other languages. The second idea to support compartmentalisation of languages at school is that it is necessary to give maximal exposure to the target language. The strong tradition of language separation is not only found in schools that teach majority languages to students who speak other home languages but also in schools aiming to develop multilingual competence in several languages. It is obvious that extended exposure to the target language(s) is necessary, but there is also a real need to build on what students already know.

Pedagogical translanguaging aims at developing multilingualism in school contexts and advocates for an integrated approach to languages. In this Element, we argue that optimising the use of the resources multilingual speakers have at their disposal can have a positive influence on students' linguistic and academic development. Languages can reinforce each other and prior linguistic knowledge is an advantage that can be used in the classroom. Another argument is that using two or more languages in the same lesson does not imply less exposure to the target language even if this is a minority language. The time allocated to activating resources from the majority language in the space of the minority language can easily be compensated for when pedagogical translanguaging is implemented across the curriculum and the minority language is also used in the majority-language lessons.

As Cenoz and Gorter (2020) explain, it sounds paradoxical to ignore and avoid the use of the multilingual students' resources by using a monolingual approach when the goal is to develop multilingual competences. The rich trajectories multilingual students often have are useful resources for learning additional languages and academic subjects. Another important reason to use multilingual resources from the whole linguistic repertoire is that it is natural for students to rely on what they already know and is at their disposal (Morales, Schissel & López-Gopar (2020); Tedick & Lyster, 2020). Students link new information to old information and pedagogical translanguaging aims at reinforcing that process. It is also natural for multilingual speakers to use languages in a flexible way and to translanguage spontaneously (García & Li, 2014; Duarte & Kirsch, 2020). Pedagogical translanguaging has as its point of reference multilingual individuals and multilingual societies because they represent the way people communicate.

Pedagogical translanguaging fosters the use of two or more languages in the same lesson; however, in this Element, the need to consider the specific learning aims and contexts is highlighted. Pedagogical translanguaging presents the framework of reference to develop an integrated approach to language and content learning. At the same time, this Element emphasises the need for tailor-made implementations that are adapted to linguistic, social and educational characteristics of each context.

Plan of the Element

After Section 1, which is the introduction, this Element is structured as follows: Section 2 'What Is Translanguaging?' analyses the original use of the term 'translanguaging' in Welsh bilingual education aimed at the development of language and academic skills and characterised by the planned use of two languages in the same class. This section also presents the extension of translanguaging to other situations inside and outside school.

Section 3 'What Is Pedagogical Translanguaging?' presents the approach called 'Focus on Multilingualism' with the three dimensions of the multilingual speaker, the multilingual repertoire and social context as the point of departure to develop pedagogical translanguaging. It also distinguishes pedagogical translanguaging from spontaneous translanguaging and provides a definition and theoretical principles. The section then goes on to discuss the core characteristics of pedagogical translanguaging.

Section 4 'Metalinguistic Awareness, Pedagogical Practices and Assessment' explains the role of metalinguistic awareness as related to pedagogical translanguaging. This section also shows pedagogical translanguaging practices and explores multilingual approaches to language and academic content assessment.

Section 5 'Minority Languages, Immersion and CLIL' acknowledges the importance of context, particularly in the case of minority languages. It highlights the importance of protecting minority languages as related to the context of pedagogical translanguaging. This section also connects minority and majority-language students by exploring the benefits of pedagogical translanguaging when they learn through the medium of a second or additional language.

Section 6 'Conclusion and Future Perspectives' summarises the key points of the Element, draws conclusions and provides future perspectives.

This Element will be of interest to researchers, graduate students and teacher educators interested in multilingual education, content and language integrated learning, content-based instruction, immersion programmes and minority languages.

2 What Is Translanguaging?

2.1 The Origin of Translanguaging

The term 'translanguaging' comes from Welsh bilingual education and was first used in the Welsh language as 'trawsieithu'. Translanguaging in the Welsh context refers to 'a pedagogical practice which deliberately switches the language mode of input and output in bilingual classrooms' (Lewis, Jones & Baker,

2012a, p. 643). Williams (1994) coined the term 'trawsieithu' in his doctoral thesis after observing some specific bilingual practices in Welsh schools. In his thesis, he provides an example of a history lesson for year 9 students (13–14 years old). Box 1 provides an example of translanguaging (authors' description of a task included in Williams, 1994, pp. 389–390).

According to Williams (1994), the diary entry is the most interesting activity because students need to read and understand the Welsh text as well as the English ones to complete the task. Williams (1994, p. 262) considers this task an example of translanguaging that is quite demanding:

> BOX 1 THE INDUSTRIAL REVOLUTION
>
> The example has five elements. There are two images (Jacob's Island and Glasgow) and three short texts about life in industrial suburbs and cities in the nineteenth century: Jacob's Island in London, Liverpool and Merthyr Tudful in Wales. The first two texts are in English and the third is in Welsh. Students have to answer five short questions, three in English about the texts written in English and two in Welsh about the text in Welsh. There is also a task asking students to write a diary entry for the 15 July 1845 imagining that they lived in an industrial town and including information about the house, street and town.

> Mae'r ddawn hon o drawsieithu sef darllen yn y naill iaith, mewnoli'r wybodaeth a'i hatgynhyrchu yn y llall yn golygu safon weithredol uchel o ddwyieithrwydd.
>
> [This skill of translanguaging, which is to read in one language, to internalize the information and to reproduce it in the other, means a high operational standard of bilingualism.]

Translanguaging has some points in common with the 'New Concurrent Approach' proposed by Jacobson (1990), but Williams (2000) explains that translanguaging needs cues to trigger language switching. Both approaches use two languages in the same class but in a completely different way. Box 2 describes an example of the New Concurrent Approach given by Jacobson (1990, p. 12).

Jacobson explains that the switching is only teacher initiated, and it has to be justified because it has a purpose. In the New Concurrent Approach, the switching of languages is at the sentence level and differs from the process of cognitive engagement that is taking place in translanguaging. Williams (2002, p. 37) refers to this cognitive engagement when he explains that in the case of translanguaging,

Box 2 Sequences of teacher-student interaction in Jacobson's example of the New Concurrent Approach using English and Spanish.

1st turn. The teacher asks two questions about the content of the previous lesson about air, weight and space. The questions are in English and the students answer in English.

2nd turn. The teacher gives feedback in English and asks another question in English. The students answer in English.

3rd turn. The teacher gives feedback in English, asks students if they remember an experiment in Spanish and then asks about the experiment in Spanish. One of the students answers in Spanish.

4th turn. The teacher gives feedback in Spanish and asks a question about the experiment in English. One of the students answers in English.

5th turn. In the last turn, the teacher uses Spanish to give feedback to the student and to explain how the experiment worked.

students process input in one language and then they switch the message/concept to the other language and they could even augment and supplement the message in the output. Baker and Wright (2017, p. 280) define translanguaging as 'the process of making meaning, shaping experiences, understandings and knowledge through the use of two languages'. Translanguaging has some specific characteristics that will be explained as follows.

2.1.1 Translanguaging Has as Its Aim the Development of Language Skills in Both Welsh and English

Williams (2002, p. 42) explains that in Wales, the aim is 'to strengthen and to use both languages to a high level in order to develop balanced and confident bilingual pupils'. He makes a distinction between this aim and the aim in the United States where 'the priority in education is to acquire the second language, English, in order to displace the vernacular language'. This statement does not apply to all US programmes, but it is important to highlight the differences between the two contexts. In the United States, translanguaging has more of a social justice focus and is seen as empowering minority students (García & Lin, 2017). Williams works in a bilingual education context where the minority language, Welsh, is promoted not only for L1 speakers but also for speakers of English or other home languages. He considers that translanguaging can use the stronger language to develop the weaker one so as to contribute towards a balanced development of the two languages. Williams (2002, p. 42) thinks that translanguaging is appropriate 'for children who have a reasonably good grasp of both languages'. His focus is mainly on students who have English as their L1 and have learned Welsh by attending bilingual schools. As he says, these students have learned Welsh at nursery and primary school, but it is important to maintain and develop Welsh along with English at secondary school (Williams, 2002). In the context of Welsh bilingual education, Welsh L1 and English L1 students are in the same class, but their percentage varies depending on the use of Welsh in the area.

The aim of translanguaging is to 'increase understanding' and 'augment the pupil's ability in both languages' (Williams 2002, p. 37). Translanguaging requires a full understanding of the language used in the input and 'sufficient vocabulary and a firm enough grasp of the other language in order to express the message' (Williams 2002, p. 37).

Baker (2003) highlighted that one of the advantages of translanguaging is that it helps develop skills in the weaker language because students have to undertake challenging tasks in both languages. In the context of Welsh bilingual education, the aim is to develop oral and literacy skills in both languages at all levels of education. The varieties used for this purpose are the standard varieties of English and Welsh. The importance of developing the minority language is at the heart of translanguaging.

2.1.2 Translanguaging Aims at Developing Academic Skills across the Curriculum

The example of translanguaging given by Williams (1994) in his thesis is from a history class (see Box 1). Translanguaging provides 'a deeper and fuller understanding of the subject matter' by developing the two languages (Baker 2003, p. 82). Baker (2000) explains that the subject matter has to be properly 'digested and reconstructed' when the two languages are used for input and output. Baker and Wright (2017, pp. 280–281) argue that translanguaging is efficient in building understanding because 'pre-existing knowledge is a foundation for further learning and there is ease of crosslinguistic transfer as two languages are interdependent'. Lewis, Jones and Baker (2012a, p. 644) emphasise how the process of translanguaging 'uses various cognitive processing skills in listening and reading, the assimilation and accommodation of information, choosing and selecting from the brain storage to communicate in speaking and writing'. The development of these skills results in a deeper understanding of content subjects than when only one language is used.

Translanguaging also offers the possibility of using more resources when teaching subject matter because it provides access to two languages, and there are more teaching materials in English than in Welsh. Williams (2002) says that translanguaging could imply more use of English textbooks and audiovisual materials in Welsh bilingual education and at the same time highlights the importance of producing teaching materials in Welsh.

2.1.3 Translanguaging Activities Are Planned and the Two Languages Are Used in the Same Session

The use of Welsh and English is planned with a systematic use of the two languages. The activities, as we have seen in the example about the industrial revolution, are designed in both languages. Baker and Wright (2017, p. 279) explain language planning at the classroom level is needed to develop the two languages and add that it is not enough to simply use the two languages. Translanguaging implies that the use of the two languages is carefully planned and that teachers are aware of the language they use for each activity. Systematic planning of the input and the output provides an opportunity to develop different skills (listening, speaking, reading, writing) in the two languages.

Using two languages in the same class session goes against the tradition of language separation and breaks the boundaries of the strict allocation of one specific language for one subject or for one day or class session. Williams (2012) is aware of the fact that he is breaking with tradition when defending translanguaging, but he also observes that translanguaging was already taking place in some schools. Apart from using different languages for input and output in the same class, Williams (2000) also considers the possibility of having a deliberate policy of using one language for some units or modules and the second language for others. As the development of the minority language is important, the use of Welsh has to be at the same or higher level as the use of English.

2.1.4 Translanguaging Can Be Found in the Natural Use of Languages by Bilinguals

Translanguaging, understood as deliberate switches of the language mode of input and output, can also be found outside the classroom. Williams (2003) provides an example of an English-speaking adult phoning a house and giving a message in English to a seven-year-old child. When the call ends, the child forwards the message to his father in Welsh, the language they use between them. Williams explains that the child has internalised the message and reformulated it using his own words in the other language, even extending the content of the message. This string of communication is a common practice in many everyday situations when the input from a speaker or the media is in one language and it is reported in another language, which is the language normally used by the interlocutors. Williams (2003) explains that this type of practice can be adapted to the school context, and he calls it translanguaging. For example, when students read a text in English and summarise it in Welsh, they need to skim the text and underline the main points; this is similar to the child who needs to understand the main points in his conversation with the English speaker. At school, students have to re-present the main points in Welsh, just as the child re-presents the conversation in Welsh when reporting it to his father. In the school context, translanguaging is usually official and planned, but there is some room for students to add and supplement information.

Williams (2012) explains that apart from official translanguaging, which is planned and systematic, natural translanguaging can also take place at school. This is the case particularly during the first terms in the first year when the students' level of Welsh is not high enough to carry out some activities, but it can also take place in oral work in pairs or groups of students later or when the teacher wants to make sure that there is full understanding. Both official and natural translanguaging can be initiated by teachers and students.

Additionally, Baker and Wright (2017, p. 283) explain that translanguaging can be complex to manage because it implies the integrated use of two languages, but they highlight its value: 'One value of the idea is that each teacher plans the strategic use of two languages, thinks consciously about the allocation of two languages in the classroom, reflects and reviews what is happening, and attempts to cognitively stimulate students by a "language provocative" and "language diversified" lesson.' Li (2018, p. 15) highlights that translanguaging as proposed by Williams and Baker is 'a process of knowledge construction that goes beyond language(s)'.

2.2 Extending Translanguaging

Garcia extended the concept of translanguaging and adapted it to the reality of bilingual education and bilingualism in the United States. García (2009, p. 45) defines translanguaging as 'multiple discursive practices in which bilinguals engage in order to make sense of their bilingual worlds'. Lewis, Jones and Baker (2012a, p. 647) say that 'the term has been generalised from school to street' and that the extension reaches all contexts of a bilingual person's life.

García (2009) refers to the discursive practices that are the normal mode of communication for bilinguals 'in the street' and are not necessarily related to school. As García (2009, p. 47) says, 'translanguaging includes but extends what others have called language use and language contact among bilinguals'. García (2009, p. 36) accepts that developing the ability to use the standard language is needed at school but advocates for the acceptance of bilingual communicative practices in education so as to enhance opportunities for language-minority children to be successful at school. We can compare the differences between the original use of translanguaging in Wales and its extension in the United States by looking at the process in both contexts (Table 1).

Table 1 shows that the processes involved in these two conceptions of translanguaging are quite different. Bilingual schools in Wales aim at the development of both Welsh and English linguistic and academic skills for children who, in most cases, have Welsh or English as their L1. Translanguaging in this context is linked to the promotion and development of Welsh as a school language, along with English. In the context of bilingualism in the United States and particularly in New York City, translanguaging refers to the spontaneous bilingual practices of emergent bilingual students. These students are often immigrants from low-income households and their communication practices usually include elements from Spanish and English or other languages. According to García (2009, pp. 307–308), 'translanguaging is indeed a powerful mechanism to construct understandings, to include others, and to mediate understandings across language groups'. Translanguaging in this context is linked to social justice and the empowerment of these students. As García and Lin (2017) explain, bilingual students are not usually allowed the full use of their linguistic repertoire and

Table 1 Translanguaging in Wales and the United States

	Translanguaging in Wales	**Translanguaging in the United States**
1.	Identify successful and planned bilingual pedagogical practices at school	Observe natural unplanned bilingual communicative practices in different contexts
2.	Define the characteristics of these practices and label them as translanguaging	Define the characteristics of these practices and label them as translanguaging
3.	Propose the extension of these practices to other bilingual classes and schools	Propose the legitimisation of these practices by accepting them at school

they are likely to participate less in class. Garcia and Sylvan (2011) report the greater success of bilinguals in English language arts and math exams in international high schools in New York City as compared with the average for bilingual students. Students in these public schools are recent immigrants who speak different languages, and they are allowed to use their first language at school. Translanguaging is accepted and encouraged by the teachers even if there is no teaching of those first languages and official exams are in English only.

García (2009, p. 32) considers that languages 'are not fixed codes by themselves; they are fluid codes framed within social practices', and the focus is on observable practices. This approach is related to Makoni and Pennycook's (2007) idea that languages are the inventions of social, cultural and political movements. García (2009, p. 35) had already explained that languages are socially constructed. There has been a development of this idea in more recent contributions with a clear rejection of the psycholinguistic conceptualisation of two separate linguistic systems (García & Li, 2014; Otheguy, García & Reid, 2015, 2019; García & Otheguy, 2020). Otheguy, García and Reid (2015, p. 283) give the following definition: 'Translanguaging is the deployment of a speaker's full linguistic repertoire without regard for watchful adherence to the socially and politically defined boundaries of named (and usually national and state) languages.'

Otheguy, García and Reid (2015, p. 297) add that the difference between monolinguals and bilinguals is only quantitative, and that monolinguals can also translanguage when they deploy 'all of the speaker's lexical and structural resources freely'. García and Otheguy (2020, p. 25) explain how there is a unitary linguistic repertoire, understood as a single aggregation of lexical and structural resources, and it is only from a social perspective that 'multilinguals may be correctly said to use many different named languages'. This position is controversial and has been criticised by MacSwan (2017), who believes that bilingual individuals have internally differentiated linguistic systems. Cummins (2017) steers a middle course between the two positions. He accepts that languages are social constructions and their boundaries are arbitrary, but he adds that it is important to consider that speakers treat them as separate and are able to identify each. People can identify most conversations as being in one or another language even if the boundaries are harder or softer depending on the social context.

A recurring theme in the study of translanguaging is the difference between translanguaging and code-switching. Code-switching was considered to be included in translanguaging (García, 2009; García & Sylvan, 2011), but García and Li (2014, p. 22) highlight the difference:

> Translanguaging differs from the notion of code-switching in that it refers not simply to a shift or a shuttle between two languages, but to the speakers' construction and use of original and complex interrelated discursive practices that cannot be easily assigned to one or another traditional definition of a language, but that make up the speakers' complete language repertoire.

As Vogel and García (2017, p.6) explain, translanguaging cannot include code-switching because the two concepts are 'epistemologically at odds'. Code-switching implies the existence of two language systems, while translanguaging implies one integrated language system.

The concept of translanguaging has been gaining ground, and different theoretical and pedagogical proposals have been made. Li (2011, p. 1223) refers to 'translanguaging space' as 'the act of translanguaging as well as a space created through translanguaging'. He considers that translanguaging is trans-formative because ' 'it creates a social space for the multilingual language user by bringing together different dimensions of their personal history, experience and environment, their attitude, belief and ideology, their cognitive and physical capacity into one coordinated and meaningful performance, and making it into a lived experience.'.

How is this interpretation of translanguaging applied to the classroom? Translanguaging pedagogy has as a starting point the language practices of bilingual learners. García, Ibarra Johnson and Seltzer (2017) identify three strands in translanguaging pedagogy: stance, design and shifts. Table 2 shows a summary of these three strands.

The first level, 'stance', is understood as teachers' beliefs. This is basic for any teaching, and it is obvious that teachers have to support translanguaging if it is going to be used in the classroom. 'Design' is closer to Williams' proposal of translanguaging as planned activities designed by the teacher but not limited to using different languages for the input and the output. Design is also close to what Cenoz and Gorter (2017) and this Element refer to as pedagogical trans-languaging and includes the design of instructional units and assessment.

Table 2 Strands in translanguaging pedagogy (based on García, Ibarra Johnson and Seltzer, 2017)

Stance	Firm belief that their students' language practices are a resource and a right
Design	Translanguaging instruction and assessment that integrate home and school language practices
Shifts	Moment-by-moment decisions that show teachers' flexibility and willingness to support students' voices

'Shifts' are not planned but happen in the classroom and are examples of spontaneous translanguaging. These shifts can be used by teachers as an instructional strategy, and they also establish students' identities (Creese & Blackledge, 2010).

2.3 Translanguaging as an Umbrella Term

The prefix 'trans' has two basic meanings: 'across' and 'beyond', and it seems that the original concept of translanguaging coined by Williams is closer to the 'across' meaning, while for García and Li (2014) it goes 'beyond' (see also Li, 2018).

Cenoz and Gorter (2020, p. 2) consider that 'translanguaging is nowadays an umbrella term that embraces a wide variety of theoretical and practical proposals'. In a similar vein, Leung and Valdés (2019, p. 359) view translanguaging as 'a multifaceted and a multilayered polysemic term'. This variety of proposals is shown when Vogel and Garcia (2017) explain that translanguaging is a theory, an approach to language pedagogy and fluid language practices used by bilingual people. Li (2018, p. 24) refers to a translanguaging instinct as a natural drive that highlights 'the multisensory and multimodal process of language learning and language use'. Jaspers (2018, p. 5) criticises the coexistence of several meanings and finds it confusing that 'translanguaging as an explanatory concept (the instinct) includes monolingual speakers but descriptively, as a label for fluid language use, excludes them'. Canagarajah (2013) proposes that the umbrella term should be 'translingual practices', and translanguaging could be included in the term.

The extension of translanguaging by Garcia and her colleagues has had an enormous impact, but it has also sparked off some controversy. One of the issues is that translanguaging is spreading without taking into consideration learning contexts involving majority-language students in immersion programmes or two-way programmes. Fortune and Tedick (2019) argue that the achievement and proficiency outcomes of immersion education based on language separation have been positive, but there is not enough research to show the advantages of translanguaging in language and content learning. Poza (2017) also highlights the need to conduct more studies on the effect of translanguaging on academic growth and critical understandings.

After looking at the origin of translanguaging and its extension, some of the main ideas will now be discussed regarding the concept of translanguaging and its use in school. The first idea is that translanguaging, understood as fluid language practices, is natural among bilinguals and multilinguals, but these practices are not necessarily the norm in all contexts (see also Ballinger, Lyster, Sterzuk & Genesee, 2017). Otheguy, García and Reid (2015, p. 297) acknowledge that 'there are no speakers, even monolingual ones, who translanguage everywhere and at all times'. In fact, it is also natural for bilingual and multilingual speakers to use only one language in some contexts.

Spontaneous language practices are complex and can be identified as translanguaging in some cases, whereas in others these practices can be clearly identified as being in one or the other language. Translanguaging practices can be the normal mode of communication in some contexts but not necessarily in all contexts. Moreover, the distance between multilingual speakers' spontaneous communicative practices and standard languages as taught in school varies in different contexts.

As we have already seen when referring to translanguaging in the United States, some positions question the existence of languages (Otheguy, García & Reid, 2015, 2019). This theoretical position is controversial (Cummins, 2021a, 2021b). As Leung and Valdés (2019, p. 359) point out, there is the mainstream theoretical position of considering languages as distinct; on the other side is the consideration of languages as 'bundles of lexical, syntactic, phonological, and orthographic features in use in specific places and times'. In this Element, we will refer to languages even though we completely agree with García (2009, p. 32) when she says that 'they are fluid codes framed within social practices'. We also agree with Cummins (2017) and Li (2018) that speakers are aware of the boundaries between languages even if those are arbitrary. Canagarajah (2013, pp. 15–16) also justifies the use of labelled languages not only for practical but also for theoretical reasons: 'While resources are mobile, they acquire labels and identities through situated uses in particular contexts and get reified through language ideologies. Therefore, labeled languages and language varieties have a reality for social groups. More significantly, they are an important form of identity for these groups.'

We view languages as social constructs and we are aware that there are no clear-cut boundaries between them, but we consider them as distinct even if their boundaries are soft and fluid (Cenoz & Gorter, 2020). Speakers can use resources from their whole linguistic repertoire, and there may be situations in which it is difficult to say whether the speaker is using one language or another. However, speakers identify different languages at the conscious level (Ortega, 2019), and languages have a social reality which is reflected in education policies (see also Cummins, 2017). An important reason to refer to different languages is the need students have to develop abilities in specific languages, as explained by García and Lin (2017, p. 127) in their assertion that 'bilingual education must develop bilingual students' ability to use language according to the rules and regulations that have been socially constructed for that particular language'.

2.4. Summary

Nowadays, translanguaging is one of the most influential concepts in bilingual and multilingual education. It was originally used in the context of Welsh bilingual education to refer to planned strategies aimed at developing proficiency in two languages. As we have seen, it is a polysemic term and its use varies in different contexts. The contribution of different translanguaging theories and research studies to the fields of multilingualism, sociolinguistics and applied linguistics challenges many traditional theoretical approaches and practices by offering new original ways of looking at language and education. This Element focuses on pedagogical translanguaging, and it is closely related to the original meaning of translanguaging and goes beyond it, as will be explained in the next section.

3 What Is Pedagogical Translanguaging?

3.1 Focus on Multilingualism

As we have already seen in Section 1, there is now a reaction against the traditional views of teaching languages based on the isolation of the target language and the reference to the ideal monolingual speaker (Cenoz & Gorter, 2013, 2015; Cummins, 2017). This critical reaction is linked to new approaches to languages, language learning and multilingualism in linguistically diverse societies.

Consistent with the new trends in multilingualism research, pedagogical translanguaging takes as its basis a focus on multilingualism. This is an approach for teaching and research in multilingual education which is an alternative to traditional perspectives that emphasise language separation, as it is shown in our video *Let's Make the Most of Multilingualism* (Cenoz & Gorter, 2018). Focus on multilingualism implies that multilinguals are different from monolinguals and are not expected to have the same level of proficiency in each of the languages in their multilingual repertoire. It also implies that the model of the monolingual native speaker is no longer valid for the multilingual and dynamic societies in the twenty-first century. Focus on multilingualism goes against traditional perspectives that emphasise language separation and aims at softening boundaries between languages so that language users make the most of their own multilingualism (Cenoz & Gorter, 2014). Focus on multilingualism has three dimensions: (i) the multilingual speaker, (ii) the multilingual repertoire, and (iii) the social context.

3.1.1 The Multilingual Speaker

The communicative skills of multilingual speakers have traditionally been measured from a monolingual perspective against the yardstick of the ideal native speaker of each of the languages involved. The idea is that learners can make progress and advance so as to get closer to the native speaker, but most of them never achieve the same level of 'nativeness' as their models. Learners are expected to make progress along what turns out to be an endless path. This situation is sometimes referred to as the 'incomplete acquisition' of the target language (Montrul & Silva-Corvalán, 2019), even though the latter concept has been severely criticised (Otheguy, 2016). In many contexts, even speakers with a high level of competence and language teachers who have learned a second or third language suffer from anxiety and low self-esteem because they are not native speakers of the language they teach (Llurda, 2014; Santos, Cenoz & Gorter, 2017).This monolingual view produces a sense of failure and lack of self-confidence when learning languages because the level to be reached in the target language is seen as an impossible goal (Cook 2010).

Focus on multilingualism proposes to consider multilingual speakers as such and not as monolingual speakers of each of the languages. The idea is to look at the different ways these speakers learn and use their languages without comparing them with ideal native speakers of different languages. It is also important to consider that the communicative competence of multilingual speakers is fluid, not fixed, difficult to measure but real. A multilingual speaker uses different languages either in isolation or mixed, for different purposes instead of using one language for all possible situations. Cook (1992) explains that multilinguals have a qualitatively different type of competence, a complex type of competence that he calls 'multicompetence'. The analysis of multilingual discourse practices also shows that multilingual speakers are different from monolingual speakers because they can use more linguistic resources to shape the communicative context (Block, 2007; Creese & Blackledge, 2010).

Multilingual speakers also have different trajectories as compared with monolingual speakers because they have experienced different linguistic situations in their lives. Their linguistic trajectories are richer and more dynamic and involve cognitive, social and emotional aspects. Trajectories influence the way multilinguals learn and use additional languages because they are shaped by experiences in their lives (Douglas Fir Group, 2016, p. 26). When multilingual speakers learn an additional language, they adjust and develop their own repertoire, and this cannot happen in the case of monolingual speakers (see also Canagarajah, 2018).

Multilingual discourses are also different from monolingual ones. Multilingual speakers use different languages depending on the context, and they can also use resources from different languages in some contexts. It can be said that multilingual speakers navigate between languages and do not use each of their languages for the same purposes in all communicative situations, in the same domains or with the same people. However, in many contexts there is still a preference for native speaker teachers, and the communicative abilities of multilingual teachers who do not have English as a first language are not fully appreciated (Llurda, 2014).

3.1.2 The Multilingual Repertoire

As we have already seen, multilingual speakers have a rich repertoire that includes not only linguistic elements but also their trajectories as language learners and language users. Focus on multilingualism considers the multilingual speaker's repertoire as a whole wherein the languages are connected to each other and support each other. There is a high degree of connectivity and dynamic interplay between the languages.

The multilingual repertoire can be a rich resource for multilinguals because they can compare elements of their different languages at different levels (phonetic, lexical, morphosyntactic, pragmatic, discursive) and use their resources crosslinguistically. The multilingual repertoire is also a resource to face different situations in communicative interaction and to use learning and communicative strategies that are part of the multilingual speaker's trajectory. Research that goes beyond two languages into third language acquisition has provided some evidence about the interaction between languages (see, for example, De Angelis, 2007; Jarvis & Pavlenko, 2008; Gabrys-Barker, 2012). Findings in this area indicate that the first and second languages can influence the third language but also that learning an additional language can have an effect on previously known languages.

The ideology of language separation does not allow multilingual speakers to make optimal use of their own multilingual resources. The idea behind focus on multilingualism is the opposite. Multilingual speakers can be more effective learners and users of a target language if they are allowed to use resources from their whole linguistic repertoire. The languages in the multilingual speakers' repertoire need to be activated to support metalinguistic reflection and the acquisition of other languages. When learning a new language, multilinguals tend naturally to use the resources they have in their multilingual repertoire, but this activation is limited and needs to be increased so that speakers maximise their multilingual skills.

3.1.3 The Social Context

Multilingual speakers acquire and use languages while engaging in language practices in a social context. Multilingualism has a social dimension, not only a linguistic one. Multilinguals use their linguistic resources in a social context and shape this context in communicative interaction (see also Canagarajah, 2007; Kramsch, 2010). Multilingual students have their own communities of practice in which they share beliefs, values, practices and ways of talking and doing things. It is in these social contexts, which include digitally mediated communication, where there are more opportunities for learners to use languages as a resource in successful communication. As Cenoz and Bereziartua (2016) report, when communicating digitally among themselves, students create their own spaces combining resources from different languages and dialects and multimodal resources (icons, different fonts and colours). In this way, they shape their own communicative context, which is different from other communicative contexts in which they may be engaged with family or at school. Multilingual speakers always have their linguistic resources available; however, depending on the social context, translanguaging practices can be more or less prominent. When students are not constrained by school regulations about language use in class, they can use their resources in more creative ways. Multilingual speakers are aware of the differences in the status and use of the languages in their repertoire in society, which also has an important role in their preferences in language use. The three dimensions of focus on multilingualism are represented by positioning the speaker and the repertoire in the centre, surrounded by the social context, as shown in Figure 1.

3.2 Definition of Pedagogical Translanguaging and Theoretical Background

Pedagogical translanguaging has been defined as 'planned by the teacher inside the classroom and can refer to the use of different languages for input and output or to other planned strategies based on the use of students' resources from the whole linguistic repertoire' (Cenoz, 2017, p. 194). As can be seen in this

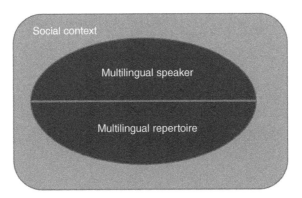

Figure 1 The three dimensions of focus on multilingualism

definition, pedagogical translanguaging mobilises the students' repertoire through instruction.

Cenoz and Gorter (2017, 2020) distinguish between pedagogical and spontaneous translanguaging. Pedagogical translanguaging is a pedagogic theory and practice that refers to instructional strategies which integrate two or more languages. Spontaneous translanguaging refers to the reality of bilingual usage in naturally occurring contexts where boundaries between languages are fluid and constantly shifting. A continuum can represent these two types of translanguaging rather than a dichotomy because there can be intermediate situations (Figure 2). Pedagogical translanguaging is designed by the teacher but can occur next to the spontaneous use of multilingual resources. Even if spontaneous translanguaging has not been planned, the teacher can link it to the learning process and it can have a clear pedagogical value (see also Lin & Lo, 2016; Lin, 2020).

Pedagogical translanguaging is a theoretical and practical approach in the context of multilingual education, that is, in schools that aim at multilingualism (Cenoz, 2009). Pedagogical translanguaging is closely related to the principles and practices of the original way translanguaging was used in Wales, as explained in Section 2 (Williams, 1994, 2002; Lewis, Jones & Baker, 2012a). The aim is to develop multilingualism in two or more languages in both language and content classes, and this includes the development of the minority language. We understand pedagogical translanguaging as including the alternation of languages in both the input and the output, but it also goes beyond the original approach of translanguaging because it includes other practices that use elements from the whole linguistic repertoire. These practices are related to the development of metalinguistic awareness by analysing and reflecting on languages as will be explained in Section 4.2. Pedagogical translanguaging applies exclusively to educational contexts and has a pedagogical purpose in that it mediates learning when multilingual resources are used (see also Ganuza & Hedman, 2017).

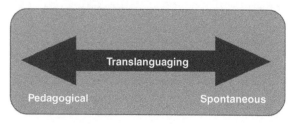

Figure 2 Pedagogical and spontaneous translanguaging

As we have already seen in the previous section, for Vogel and Garcia (2017) translanguaging is a theory, an approach to language pedagogy and fluid language practices used by bilingual people. Regarding its scope, pedagogical translanguaging is focused on the school context and learning languages and content; so in this sense, it is not as broad as the concept of translanguaging used by García and Li (2014. p. 2) or Vogel and Garcia (2017). However, pedagogical translanguaging is broad in the sense that it applies to a wider population and not only to bilingual students in contexts where spontaneous translanguaging is very common. Pedagogical translanguaging is also broad because it is not limited to two languages but extends to three or more languages. Pedagogical translanguaging is concerned with the planning, application and extension of multilingual pedagogical strategies and practices based on the student's whole linguistic repertoire. It can be designed at the phonetic, lexical, morphosyntactic, pragmatic and discourse levels and can be implemented in language classes and content classes including oral and written activities (see Leonet, Cenoz & Gorter, 2017; Cenoz & Santos, 2020).

Pedagogical translanguaging as an approach is based on theoretical principles and learning theories that can promote the development of multilingualism. In the following section, we look at some theoretical concepts that are relevant to the development and implementation of pedagogical translanguaging. First, we will look at the concept of prior knowledge, then at scaffolding and finally at connected growers.

3.2.1 Prior Knowledge

Pedagogical translanguaging is based on how learning occurs and prior knowledge or pre-existing knowledge is recognised as essential. In the volume *How People Learn* edited by Brandsford and colleagues and published by the National Research Council in 2000, it is formulated as follows: 'There is a good deal of evidence that learning is enhanced when teachers pay attention to the knowledge and beliefs that learners bring to a learning task, use this knowledge as a starting point for new instruction, and monitor students' changing conceptions as instruction proceeds' (Bransford, Brown & Cocking, 2000, p. 11).

Prior knowledge is pre-existing information held by the students because of their previous experience and includes their cultural and social knowledge based on their social roles (Bransford, Brown & Cocking, 2000, pp. 71–2). Prior knowledge already exists in the case of multilingual learners, and pedagogical translanguaging places the learner at the centre of the teaching and learning process and uses pre-existing knowledge as a resource. From the perspective of pedagogical translanguaging, prior knowledge does not only refer to the knowledge of vocabulary or grammar in different languages but also to the knowledge of pragmatic and social aspects of language use. Prior knowledge also includes beliefs about languages and metalinguistic awareness, that is, awareness about how languages work.

The knowledge learners bring to the classroom may not exactly match what the teacher intends to teach, but its activation can help relate that pre-existing knowledge to the new information. As Kostons and Van der Werf (2015) explain, prior knowledge is not automatically activated and facilitating its activation can have a positive effect on learning. A basic idea in pedagogical translanguaging is the activation of the knowledge multilingual learners have acquired as the result of their experience of using several languages. Learners may have the knowledge, but it is crucial to reinforce their access to that knowledge. If prior knowledge of linguistic resources is suppressed, learning can be less effective. Gollub et al. (2002) consider that prior knowledge is one of the basic learning principles and that when prior knowledge is not engaged, students are likely to fail to understand what teachers explain in class. They add: 'Effective teaching involves gauging what learners already know about a subject and finding ways to build on that knowledge' (Gollub et al. 2002, p. 121).

Prior knowledge is important in many theoretical approaches to learning, including constructivism, constructionism, cognitivism and postmodern theories of learning. Pedagogical translanguaging aims at bridging the gap between prior knowledge and the development of language and academic skills.

3.2.2 Scaffolding

Scaffolding has been defined as a 'process that enables a child or novice to solve a problem, carry out a task or achieve a goal which would be beyond his unassisted efforts' (Wood, Bruner & Ross. 1976, p. 90). Although Wood, Bruner and Ross (1976) refer to assistance to a child by an adult, scaffolding is used in different learning contexts at different ages and includes assistance by computer-based tools. Swain and Lapkin (2013, p. 119) adapt this definition to the context of immersion education, stating that 'a more expert learner or a teacher helps another person to go beyond what he/she can do alone in, for example, linguistic expression, conceptual understanding, or performing an action'. Scaffolding is closely associated to the Vygotskian concept of the zone of proximal development (ZPD) in sociocultural theory. Swain and Suzuki (2008) consider the ZPD to be the distance between an individual's independent abilities to solve a problem and the potential abilities if the individual is guided by another person or by tools. Swain and Lapkin (2013) hold the view that sociocultural theory provides a basis to support the use of the L1 in immersion programmes and they propose the three guiding principles stated in Table 3.

Swain and Lapkin (2013) consider that the L1 is an important cognitive tool that when necessary should be allowed as a mediating tool. It helps learners scaffold their understanding, but when their proficiency in the L2 increases, learners should be encouraged to use their L2. As Walqui (2006, p. 169) explains, 'scaffolds are by definition temporary' (see also Walqui & Van Lier, 2010).

Scaffolding is often associated with sociocultural theory, but it is also an important concept in dynamic systems theory. As Van Geert and Steenbeek (2005, p. 117) state, 'Scaffolding is an intrinsically dynamic notion. It describes how a particular level of knowledge or skill in a student changes as a result of the scaffolding process.' Kupers, Van Dijk and Van Geert (2017) explain that scaffolding is connected to students' agency and autonomy because students are active participants and they are expected to assume responsibility for their own learning.

In the context of language learning and multilingual education, allowing for flexible language practices to scaffold the transition to the use of majority language at school has often been considered one of the main functions of translanguaging in different contexts. For example, Duarte (2020) reports two studies carried out in Luxembourg and the Netherlands and found that translanguaging can be a bridge for immigrant children because it fulfills 'a scaffolding function offering temporary bridges between languages which allow pupils to build links between official instruction languages and between home and school languages' (p. 243). In a different context, where the school has students with different first languages but does not aim at multilingualism, Daniel et al. (2019) show how translanguaging can also be used for scaffolding when students use their home languages in an English-only school in the United

Table 3 Sociocultural theory: Guiding principles to use the L1 in immersion programmes (based on Swain & Lapkin, 2013)

1. To understand and generate complex ideas when students are working on an oral or written task in the target language.
2. To create a secure classroom environment so that students are confident and ready to interact.
3. The L1 should be used with a purpose, particularly for crosslinguistic comparisons or to make abstract vocabulary comprehensible.

States. In the context of Chinese language teaching in Hong Kong, Wang (2019) found that translanguaging was 'one of the most effective and efficient systems of scaffolding for classroom learning' (p. 75). Vaish (2020) also reports some translanguaging practices that are used as a scaffold in the context of learning English in Singapore.

García and Li (2014) say that translanguaging is used as a scaffold but explain that translanguaging is more than scaffolding. Menken and Sánchez (2019) add that in the United States, it cannot be just a transition to learn English; it should result in dynamic bilingualism.

Scaffolding is very important in pedagogical translanguaging not as a transition to develop proficiency in the majority language but as a way of developing the multilingual repertoire. Scaffolding in pedagogical translanguaging refers to the development of skills and strategies that enable students to use their resources as multilingual speakers. Scaffolding has a bridging function as proposed by Walqui (2006) because it links prior knowledge to new information so that learners realise that there are connections between languages. Pedagogical translanguaging is also a scaffold to develop metalinguistic awareness, as will be seen in Section 4.

3.2.3 Connected Growers

The concept of 'connected growers' is used in dynamic systems theory to explain learning and development (Van Geert 1994). This theory has also been applied to language learning and multilingualism and considers language development as a complex, nonlinear dynamic process (Herdina & Jessner, 2002; De Bot, Lowie & Verspoor, 2007; Larsen-Freeman, 2007). According to Van Geert (2003), each component of the linguistic system, such as the lexicon or the syntax, is subject to growth and is called a 'grower'. Growers can be connected to each other and can be in a supporting or competitive relationship, and the support or competition can be strong or weak (Van Geert, 1994).

De Bot, Lowie and Verspoor (2007) explain that one example of connected growers could be the relationship between the development of listening comprehension and the lexicon in second language acquisition. These two growers reinforce each other because increased listening comprehension can support the development of the lexicon, and increased knowledge of vocabulary can support a higher ability in listening comprehension. De Bot, Lowie and Verspoor (2007) add that subsystems need resources to grow, but connected growers that support each other need fewer resources than growers that are not connected to each other. Spoelman and Verspoor (2010) analysed fifty-four writing samples from an adult Dutch learner of Finnish over three years. They identified connected growers that supported each other between both word complexity and noun phrase complexity and word complexity and sentence complexity. Verspoor, Lowie and van Dijk (2008) found that two other complexity measures, finite verb ratio and noun phrase length, were connected growers.

The analysis of connected growers from the perspective of dynamic systems theory offers interesting insights in the study of language development but looks at the second or additional language rather than at the whole multilingual repertoire. If we use a multilingual lens, the identification of connected growers can be applied across languages. Cenoz and Gorter (2011) reported that learners use similar strategies in the organisation of content and in the structure of compositions written in three languages. This indicates that students are developing writing skills in the three languages and that these skills are connected to one another. It could be argued that the growth of skills to organize content or to structure a text in one language is connected to the development of these skills in the other two languages. Longitudinal studies showing the development of these skills at different times in the three languages could confirm that they are connected growers. Connected growers could exist not only at the discourse level but also in the acquisition of other language skills. Pedagogical translanguaging aims at identifying connected growers, that is, growers that support each other and imply the use of fewer resources and more efficient development of the multilingual repertoire.

3.3 Core Characteristics of Pedagogical Translanguaging

Cenoz and Gorter (2020) explain that pedagogical translanguaging can take many shapes, but it also shares some core characteristics (Table 4).

Regarding the *type of programme*, pedagogical translanguaging is very broad, but it takes place in programmes that focus on activating the multilingual repertoire. These programmes can be found in the context of bilingual and multilingual education, which aims at developing language and literacy in two or more languages. The programmes can be immersion programmes,

Table 4 Core characteristics of pedagogical translanguaging

Type of programme	Multilingual education and second/additional language education
Type of student	Multilingual or emergent multilingual
Aims	Linguistic and academic development
Organisation	Planned, designed
Approach	Multilingual/heteroglossic

minority-language reinforcement programmes or content and language integrated programmes, among others. The key idea is that there is no replacement of one language by another and that translanguaging is not a scaffold to shift from the minority to the majority language. Multilingual education programmes can be found in many parts of the world, including immersion and CLIL programmes as well as Welsh bilingual education, where the original concept of translanguaging was developed. Multilingual education can also apply to programmes that include three or more languages, such as multilingual programmes in the Basque Country, China or Mexico (Gorter, Zenotz & Cenoz, 2014). Pedagogical translanguaging can also take place in second and additional language education programmes, provided that the focus is on developing the students' multilingual repertoire.

As far as the *type of student* is concerned, pedagogical translanguaging is aimed at multilingual or emergent multilingual students, that is, students who are multilingual or are in the process of becoming multilingual. The students can be speakers of a regional minority language, an immigrant minority language or a majority language. In the case of minority-language speakers, it is likely that students have already had exposure to the majority language outside school. Pedagogical translanguaging can apply to different school grades and levels of multilingual competence.

Pedagogical translanguaging *aims* at the development of school languages and academic content. It supports the learning of weaker languages, which can be minority languages or languages not widely used in society, by using the multilingual speaker's resources. The idea is to maximise the learner's linguistic resources as a multilingual when developing language and academic subjects. Students activate prior knowledge to maximise the use of their resources as multilingual speakers. They need pedagogical translanguaging as a scaffold to become aware of those resources and activate connected growers that go across languages. In this way, they can develop metalinguistic awareness and lay the foundation for autonomous learning. Pedagogical translanguaging works on multilingual resources and, in the case of content, the activation of prior knowledge goes beyond language, as will be seen in Section 5. However, content is learned through language(s), and pedagogical translanguaging can contribute to the comprehension of academic content. Pedagogical translanguaging has as a core characteristics that it aims at linguistic and academic development because it can be applied both in language and content subjects.

In relation to *organisation*, the characteristic of pedagogical translanguaging is that it is planned and designed by the teacher as part of his/her lesson plan. It goes beyond allowing for the flexible use of languages. Pedagogical translanguaging implies a definition of the objectives for each lesson, the selection of material, and the specific didactics to carry out the learning tasks and teaching activities. One of the characteristics of pedagogical translanguaging is that it uses multilingual resources from the whole repertoire in the same lesson. In this sense, it goes beyond the use of planning coordinated activities in different language classes, such as bilingual read-aloud projects in French immersion classes (Lyster, Collins & Ballinger, 2009; Lyster, Quiroga & Ballinger, 2013). Pedagogical translanguaging uses two or more languages in the same class, but it goes beyond the original concept of translanguaging in Wales of alternating the input and the output by using other strategies and activities. Pedagogical translanguaging is learner centred and takes the multilingual speaker and his/her repertoire as the starting point. The learner is a person who uses languages in a social context, and pedagogical translanguaging promotes learner agency so that he/she takes an active role and learns to become autonomous regarding the use of his/her own multilingual resources.

As far as *approach* is concerned, pedagogical translanguaging is multilingual and heteroglossic. It views languages as dynamic and co-existing; by focusing on the whole multilingual repertoire, it looks at the activation of multiple languages, varieties, registers and other signs from multilingual speakers. As we have already seen in Section 2, we refer to languages because even though they are social constructs, they are identified as such by speakers and therefore have a social reality. Boundaries between languages are soft and elements from several languages can be used in a dynamic way in class. Multilingual speakers are different from monolingual speakers because they have an integrated knowledge of their languages (Cook & Bassetti, 2005), but traditional approaches have not acknowledged the differences and have blocked the resources multilingual speakers can use when learning languages and content at school. By softening the boundaries between languages, resources from the whole linguistic repertoire can be used in the same class.

3.4 Summary

In this section, pedagogical translanguaging has been defined and its core characteristics have been explained. Pedagogical translanguaging takes the focus on multilingualism as its point of departure, and it is also based on the concepts of prior knowledge, scaffolding and connected growers. Pedagogical translanguaging can take different forms and varies across contexts, but it aims at linguistic and academic development in the context of multilingual education by activating multilingual speakers' resources. A core characteristic of pedagogical translanguaging is that it is planned. The next section will look at metalinguistic awareness, pedagogical translanguaging practices and assessment.

4 Metalinguistic Awareness, Pedagogical Translanguaging Practices and Assessment

4.1 Metalinguistic Awareness

One of the aims of pedagogical translanguaging is to enhance metalinguistic awareness so that multilingual speakers benefit from their own multilingualism. Figure 3 shows how the resources multilingual speakers have can influence the development of multilingual competence through metalinguistic awareness. Pedagogical translanguaging has two roles: (i) to influence the development of metalinguistic awareness by enhancing an optimal use of multilingual resources and (ii) to influence metalinguistic awareness so that it results in increased multilingual competence.

Multilingualism has been associated with enhanced metalinguistic awareness in studies on the outcomes of bilingualism, particularly when explaining the positive influence of bilingualism on third language acquisition (see for example Cenoz 2003, 2013; Rauch, Naumann & Jude, 2011). The positive association of multilingualism with metalinguistic awareness can be explained because the multilingual speakers' repertoire is broader and has more resources, and this prior knowledge can be used when a third language is acquired. Moreover, many multilinguals have more expertise as language learners because they have learned other languages apart from their first language. When learning a third or additional language, multilingual speakers can apply metalinguistic strategies that they have already developed

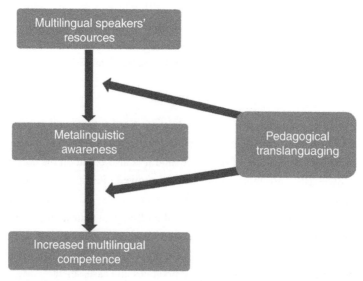

Figure 3 Pedagogical translanguaging and metalinguistic awareness

previously (see also Lasagabaster, 1998; Jessner, 2006, 2008; Izadi & Yarahmadzehi, 2020).

Even though advantages are associated with multilingualism, research studies show that students do not use all the opportunities to benefit from their multilingual resources (Otwinowska, 2016; Woll, 2018). Pedagogical translanguaging can make learners aware of their own resources and teach them to reflect on those resources by developing metalinguistic awareness.

Metalinguistic awareness has been defined in different ways. In an early study on the outcomes of bilingualism, Thomas (1988, p. 531) defined metalinguistic awareness as 'an individual's ability to focus attention on language as an object in and of itself, to reflect upon language, and to evaluate it'. The idea of focusing on language as an object is also part of the definition given by Jessner (2006, p. 42), who says that metalinguistic awareness 'refers to the ability to focus attention on language as an object in itself or to think abstractly about language, and, consequently, to play with or manipulate language'. These definitions have two main focuses. One is reflection on language that involves abstract thinking so as to try to see how language works, and the other is related to action because there is an evaluation and/or manipulation of language. These two ideas are also present in the definition given by Falk, Lindqvist and Bardel (2015, p. 229), who define it as 'the capacity to reflect upon and manipulate linguistic features, rules or data'.

In the context of multilingual education and language learning, metalinguistic awareness can be considered as part of metacognition. Metacognition refers to the awareness of one's learning or thinking processes, and metalinguistic awareness can be viewed as a subfield because it refers to the reflection on the processes related to language (Rutgers & Evans, 2017). At the same time, metalinguistic awareness is a broader concept than crosslinguistic awareness. Angelovska and Hahn (2014, p. 187) consider that in the case of crosslinguistic awareness, the focus of attention and reflection is 'upon language(s) in use and through establishing similarities and differences among the languages in one's multilingual mind'. Figure 4 shows how the three constructs could be represented as three concentric circles, where the outer circle is metacognitive awareness, the middle circle metalinguistic awareness and the inner circle crosslinguistic awareness. Pedagogical translanguaging focuses mainly on raising crosslinguistic awareness, but it can also develop other areas of metalinguistic awareness.

Metalinguistic awareness has also been compared with metalinguistic knowledge. Metalinguistic knowledge refers to the ability to reflect on language(s), but the knowledge has to be explicit and verbalised (Bialystok & Barac 2012; Falk et al. 2015; Angelovska 2018). Metalinguistic awareness

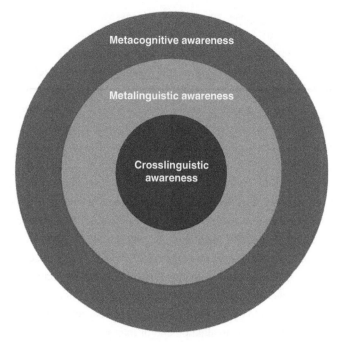

Figure 4 Metacognitive awareness, metalinguistic awareness and
crosslinguistic awareness

does not necessarily imply depth of analysis, but the distinction between the
two is not always obvious. Woll (2018) provides examples of three degrees of
awareness following the proposal made by Leow (1997), who distinguished
cognitive change, meta-awareness and morphological rule (see Table 5). The
examples are learning the German words 'Herz, Stein, Gast and seltener'
(Woll 2018, p. 184–5).

We can see that in the case of 'Herz' (cognitive change), there is no deep
analysis but just an association with an English word. In the case of 'Stein'
(meta-awareness), there is some reflection about the names of cities; in the
case of 'Gast' and 'seltener', there is explicit metalinguistic knowledge and
reference to a grammatical category. Pedagogical translanguaging can be
applied to the three levels, and the need for metalinguistic knowledge will
depend on the students' school grade and their prior knowledge. It is possible
to use elements of the multilingual repertoire by focusing on a word,
a structure or a discourse marker but without a high level of reflection and
very limited metalinguistic knowledge. However, a higher level of metalinguistic awareness can help make associations with prior knowledge (Jessner,
2006; Woll, 2018).

Table 5 Metalinguistic awareness and metalinguistic knowledge (based on Woll 2018)

Metalinguistic awareness	Cognitive change	*This makes me think of 'heart', as in 'heart' [in English], Herz*
Metalinguistic knowledge	Meta-awareness	*'Stein' It must be a place, many cities end in 'stein'*
	Morphological rule	*'Gast' must be 'guest' and 'seltener' that must be the adjective that goes with it*

Metalinguistic awareness and crosslinguistic awareness are not limited to the traditional levels of language (phonology, vocabulary, morphology, syntax), and they can also apply to pragmatics and discourse. Pedagogical translanguaging uses resources from the whole multilingual repertoire, including languages that are distant because they have different origins and degrees of similarity. According to Huang (2018), learners may be more motivated to develop metalinguistic awareness when there are greater differences between the languages in their linguistic repertoire and the target language.

4.2 Pedagogical Translanguaging Practices

The multilingual repertoire can be a rich resource for multilingual speakers, but prior knowledge needs to be activated so as to develop metalinguistic awareness and specifically, crosslinguistic awareness. Multilingualism has some communicative advantages because it provides access to information and interaction in different languages. As we have seen in Section 2, Williams (2002) explained that there was more access to information when textbooks and audiovisual materials are in Welsh and English than when only one language is used in the classroom. There is also more access to interaction, as can be seen in activities proposed by García, Ibarra Johnson and Seltzer (2017), which include interviewing community leaders and parents in English, Spanish or bilingually in the US context. Pedagogical translanguaging has a specific focus on language learning, but it is broad because it can be applied to any school context where languages or content are learned through the medium of a second or additional language. It shares many practices based on the use of the whole linguistic repertoire with García, Ibarra Johnson and Seltzer's (2017) translanguaging pedagogy, but, as has already been seen in Section 2, the latter is linked to the specific context of educating students labeled English Language Learners in the United States and emphasises social justice among its aims.

As we have seen in the previous section, pedagogical translanguaging is closely related to the concepts of 'prior knowledge', 'scaffolding' and 'connected growers'. Pedagogical translanguaging embraces different pedagogical practices, but they all use resources from the students' whole linguistic repertoire and are planned by the teacher with a pedagogical purpose.

Table 6 shows different pedagogical translanguaging practices that can be regarded as strong or weak forms depending on the degree of pedagogical intervention that takes place in the process of learning and the use of two or more languages in the same class session. The practice called 'enhancing metalinguistic awareness' is the strongest and 'translanguaging shifts' the weakest. The specific characteristics of each of these practices are described as follows:

Table 6 Pedagogical translanguaging practices

Practice	Type	Sample/illustrative activities
Enhancing metalinguistic awareness	Pedagogical	Students use two or more languages in the same class and focus on analysing and reflecting on languages crosslinguistically.
Use of whole linguistic repertoire	Pedagogical	Students are encouraged to use two or more languages in the same class to carry out different activities: find sources in different languages, change language for input and output, etc.
Integrated language curriculum	Pedagogical	Students only use the target language in class. The syllabuses of the language classes are coordinated so that languages reinforce each other.
Translanguaging shifts	Spontaneous-Pedagogical	Students ask for the translation of a word they do not understand when reading a text. The teacher translates the word or gives a short explanation in a language that is not the language of instruction for the class.

Enhancing Metalinguistic Awareness. This practice is a strong form of pedagogical translanguaging because it works on reflecting on language and also because it uses two or more languages for the activities in the same class. Enhancing metalinguistic awareness practices aims to develop metalinguistic awareness by activating prior knowledge and identifying connected growers so that students can make more progress in the development of their multilingual skills. Students are asked to focus on specific aspects of the language by looking at similarities and differences in skills or language levels. Leonet, Cenoz and Gorter (2020) report a study aimed at the development of metalinguistic awareness and strategies to improve the comprehension and production of vocabulary by comparing derivatives and compounds in Basque, Spanish and English. The results of the study indicate that pedagogical translanguaging has a positive influence on morphological awareness and also on the perception multilingual students have of their multilingual repertoire.

Galante (2020a) examined the effect of pedagogical translanguaging on vocabulary by comparing the results of two groups of adult students of English in Canada. Students in one group carried out some tasks on idioms and discourse markers through translanguaging practices and students in the other group monolingually in English. The results show that participants who had engaged in pedagogical translanguaging practices obtained significantly higher scores than students in the comparison group.

Another example that has been used in Basque schools focuses on working at the discourse level in reading and writing as reported by Cenoz and Santos (2020). Secondary school students worked in groups and were given newspapers in the four languages in the curriculum so as to identify the main parts of a piece of news. After reading, writing and listening to news items in Basque, Spanish and English, students worked with a text in English and identified cognates in Basque, Spanish and French.

In another activity, students focused on the content and organisation of a request letter in Basque, Spanish and English by analysing similarities and differences and looking at the structure of the texts. They then wrote letters in the three languages. In English, their third or additional language, the letter was shorter but included all the elements of content and organisation used for the other two languages.

Enhancing metalinguistic awareness practices implies the use of the whole linguistic repertoire and can be regarded as a strong form of intervention because it focuses on language. García, Ibarra Johnson and Seltzer (2017) also provide some examples of enhancing metalinguistic awareness among their translanguaging objectives, such as the linguistic analysis of bilingual texts.

Use of Whole Linguistic Repertoire. The use of the whole linguistic repertoire is also a strong form of pedagogical translanguaging because it uses two or more languages for activities in the same class, but it is not as strong as enhancing metalinguistic awareness practices because the intervention does not focus on reflecting on language. Students are encouraged to use their multilingual repertoire for a pedagogical purpose in different ways. One possibility is to use different languages for input and output as was proposed by Williams (2002) in Wales. In this case, students either watch a video or read a text in one language and then discuss it or produce some oral or written output in the other.

Swain and Lapkin (2013) also propose the use of two languages in the same class in immersion programmes because the first language can be used as a scaffold, particularly when students have to understand and generate complex ideas. Swain and Lapkin (2013) do not refer to this practice as translanguaging, but it can be considered as such.

García, Ibarra Johnson and Seltzer (2017) provide several examples of use of the whole linguistic repertoire. Students analyse bilingual public service announcements (PSAs). They can also write bilingual PSAs in different formats (posters, short dramatic plays, oral presentations) and explain their choices. These activities can be considered examples of pedagogical translanguaging because they aim at expanding the students' multilingual repertoire and support comprehension (see also Vogel & García, 2017).

Integrated Language Curriculum. This practice implies that even if there are two or more languages in the school curriculum, they are used separately in different classes. It can be regarded as a weaker form of translanguaging because there are separate instructional spaces for each language. Integrated language curriculum implies that language subjects (Spanish, English, French, etc.) are linked to one another because of similar methodological approaches and coordination among teachers. These approaches provide space for focusing on crosslinguistic similarities and differences in the individual languages. Integrated language curriculum is a translanguaging practice that targets efficient language learning through the coordination of activities in different language classes. Apraiz Jaio, Pérez Gómez and Ruiz Pérez (2012) report communicative group projects carried out in the Basque, Spanish and English classes in primary and secondary schools. One example is a project on the topic of journalism aimed at understanding and producing narrative texts in the three languages. Students carry out specific oral and written activities in several class sessions in each of the three languages, producing a radio news broadcast in Basque, a newspaper report in Spanish and a digital story in English. There is coordination among the activities in the three languages and cross-references to the materials so that students apply what they learn in one language to the other languages. Most activities are in one language only, but in some cases it is necessary to use information from activities in one language to complete activities in the other language. Only a limited number of activities could be considered as practicing enhancing metalinguistic awareness (Table 6), such as an exercise asking students to write down the number of syllables for some cognates in the three languages. The majority of the activities are only in one language; for this reason, integrated language curriculum can be regarded as a weaker form of pedagogical translanguaging.

Cummins (2007) refers to coordination between teachers of French and English when students write stories or carry out group projects in the two languages. Lyster, Quiroga and Ballinger (2013) report a study focusing on the development of morphological awareness in French and English. The focus on derivation and decomposition is clearly related to the practice we call enhancing metalinguistic awareness, but there were separate spaces and different teachers for the two languages. This practice can be considered to be integrated language curriculum because it was based on the coordination of the activities in both language classes so as to develop crosslinguistic awareness.

Translanguaging Shifts. 'Translanguaging shifts' is a term used by García, Ibarra Johnson and Seltzer (2017) to refer to unplanned decisions that respond to communicative needs in the classroom. As we can see in Table 6, students can ask to translate a word so as to understand a text. It is not included in the lesson plan and in this sense it is spontaneous translanguaging. However, the teacher could use the opportunity to add an explanation about the word and to link it to the planned syllabus, thus building bridges between spontaneous and pedagogical translanguaging. For this reason, we consider that translanguaging shifts can be placed towards the middle of the pedagogical-spontaneous continuum, which was explained in Section 3. These shifts start as spontaneous, they have a pedagogical value and in many cases they may be linked to pedagogical translanguaging.

The four types of practices that we have described here are not sealed compartments, and different practices often take place in the same class. Pedagogical translanguaging practices do not occur in all classes or for all activities. There can be great diversity regarding the intensity of these practices depending on the educational context and the aims of the programme. In some contexts, pedagogical translanguaging practices can be limited to a few hours in the language class for a limited period of time. In other contexts, they can take many hours and become an integral part of the curriculum going across several subjects during the whole academic year. In the original proposal of translanguaging, input was in one language and output in another. In the case of pedagogical translanguaging, input and output can be in one or more languages. For example, there can be audiovisual materials with subtitles in other languages or bilingual and multilingual texts as inputs or outputs.

The need to activate the whole linguistic repertoire and the recognition of multilingual practices is gaining ground even though languages have been traditionally considered as separate systems in school contexts. According to the Common European Framework of Reference for Languages (Council of Europe, 2001, p. 4), multilinguals develop 'a unique competence to which all knowledge and experience of language contributes and in which languages interrelate and interact'.

4.3 Assessment and Pedagogical Translanguaging

Assessment is an integral part of education. In this section, multilingual and translanguaging perspectives on assessment are discussed. Large-scale standardised assessment is usually administered in one language, but there have been some multilingual approaches to assessment particularly in the case of classroom-based assessment (De Backer, Van Avermaet & Slembrouck, 2017). Regarding pedagogical translanguaging, assessment can be approached from different perspectives.

A number of studies have used a multilingual approach when assessing students (Shohamy & Menken, 2015; Gorter & Cenoz, 2017; De Backer, Slembrouck & Van Avermaet, 2019; Schissel, Leung & Chalhoub-Deville, 2019). Within this approach there are different possibilities. One of these possibilities is to provide access to texts in the first language to obtain a deeper knowledge of subject content. For example, Schissel et al. (2018) reported a study conducted in Mexico comparing two writing tasks in English. Students had to synthesise three readings when writing a letter or an email in English. Two of the readings were in English and one in Spanish in one task, while in the other task the three readings were in English. Students obtained significantly higher scores in the task that included the text in Spanish.

Heugh et al. (2017) reported a study based on a large-scale evaluation conducted in South Africa. This is one of the few examples of multilingual tests in standardised assessment. Heugh et al. (2017) reported that in a large-scale evaluation, some of the mathematics tests were presented in three languages: isiXhosa, English and Afrikaans. They observed that more than 85 percent of the students who used translations found them useful. Shohamy (2011) reported the results of a study conducted with former USSR students who had immigrated to Israel. She found that students who were given instructions in Russian and Hebrew obtained higher scores in mathematics than students who only received instructions in Hebrew.

An important perspective when assessing pedagogical translanguaging is to consider the whole linguistic repertoire and not only the skills in one language. In this way, the focus is on what students can achieve as a whole and not only in specific languages. An important step in the assessment of writing is that of Escamilla et al. (2013), who developed a rubric to assess writing skills in English and Spanish. The rubric has a quantitative and a qualitative component. The quantitative analysis looks at content, structural elements and spelling in the two languages. The texts in the two languages are evaluated side by side, and the scoring sheet has the scores for the two languages. The qualitative analysis looks at bilingual strategies that go across languages. The advantage of this rubric is that the students' performance in both languages is seen at the same time instead of only in one language at a time. As Roy (2016, p. 235) suggests, if we do not assess bilinguals in two languages, 'we will get an incomplete picture of the bilingual's knowledge'.

García, Ibarra Johnson and Seltzer (2017) present a series of translanguaging assessment tools for language and content. These tools include the teacher's assessment, student self-assessment, peer assessment and family assessment. An important point is that the idea of assessing the whole linguistic repertoire is present but goes one step further by distinguishing between 'general linguistic performance' using all language resources and 'language specific performance' in English or in LOTE (languages other than English).

Another way to consider the whole linguistic repertoire in assessment is to use a multilingualism index to compute test scores. Cenoz, Arocena and Gorter (2013) evaluated writing skills in Basque, Spanish and English separately by using a rubric based on Jacobs et al. (1981). They created two indexes, one for bilingualism, adding up the scores for Basque and Spanish, and another one for multilingualism, adding up the results of the three languages. In this way, they could see the overall multilingual competence using a different lens than when the scores in each language were considered separately.

The Council of Europe has also developed some tools that take into consideration the whole linguistic repertoire. One of them is the Language Passport, based on a self-assessment of different languages so as to provide an overview of an individual's proficiency in different languages (Council of Europe, 2011). The more recent companion volume (Council of Europe, 2018, pp. 160–2) goes further and uses specific descriptors of the multilingual repertoire for comprehension and interaction. These descriptors deal specifically with flexible alternation between languages in comprehension and production.

The assessment of pedagogical translanguaging can also focus on metalinguistic awareness looking at the way students have activated their multilingual repertoire using resources across languages in reading comprehension or writing. Another possibility is to explore the effect of pedagogical translanguaging on language and content learning by comparing pedagogical translanguaging to other approaches. A crucial aspect when assessing pedagogical translanguaging is students' reflection and self-evaluation during the learning process as part of formative assessment.

In this section, we have looked at some developments regarding assessment from a pedagogical translanguaging perspective. The steps given so far are still small and in most cases, particularly in the case of standardised assessment, only one language is used in examinations (García & Li, 2014; Slembrouck & Rosiers, 2018). An important issue is that there is very little development on the way multilingual speakers communicate by using their linguistic resources together. Slembrouck, Van Avermaet and Van Gorp (2018) explain that limitation: 'We tested reading comprehension in Turkish and Dutch, and we did so separately following the logic and practice of large-scale standardized testing. The larger realization is that we still appear to be quite a few steps removed from adequately conceptualizing an assessment of multilingual proficiency.' A few steps have been taken when including the use of different resources in assessment (García, Ibarra Johnson & Seltzer, 2017) or descriptors about flexible alternation between languages (Council of Europe, 2018), but there is a real need to replace monolingual approaches to assessment with multilingual ones (Roy, 2016; Gorter & Cenoz, 2017; Hofer & Jessner, 2019; Galante, 2020b).

4.4 Summary

Multilingual students have resources in their multilingual repertoire, but these resources often need to be activated so that they develop metalinguistic awareness and improve their multilingual competence. Pedagogical translanguaging practices can have different degrees of intensity depending on their focus on metalinguistic awareness and the use of different languages in the same class. Assessment based on multilingual and translanguaging pedagogies can take various shapes depending on context. In the next section, the role of context is discussed as related to pedagogical translanguaging by looking at the status of languages in the curriculum and their use as languages of instruction.

5 Minority Languages, Immersion and CLIL

5.1 The Diversity of Educational Contexts

Since its origin in the context of Welsh-English bilingual education, translanguaging has been examined in many diverse contexts in different parts of the world. One of the sources of diversity is student background (Cenoz & Gorter, 2020).

Students may use a minority language as a home language, which could be a regional minority or an immigrant language, or they might use the majority language of a given sociolinguistic context as their home language. Minority-language students can be speakers of a regional language and attend bi/multilingual education programmes to maintain and reinforce the minority language, as is the case for Welsh L1 speakers in Wales or Basque L1 speakers in the Basque Country. In some cases, minority-language speakers are enrolled in programmes that aim at shifting towards the majority language and not at developing the minority language. This is often the case of immigrant students in different parts of the world.

Translanguaging can also take place when students are speakers of the majority language and are learning another language in immersion and CLIL programmes. This is often the case in Welsh bilingual schools with students who have English as their first language and use Welsh as a language of instruction. This is also the case for speakers of Spanish in multilingual programmes in the Basque Country, for speakers of English in immersion programmes in Canada or the United States or for L1 speakers of Chinese in CLIL English programmes in China. These are only some examples related to student background and the diversity of situations in which pedagogical translanguaging can take place. The diversity is also due to educational variables, such as the number and status of the different languages in the curriculum or teaching strategies which include translanguaging practices. In the next section, we will look at pedagogical translanguaging involving minority languages followed by a section on immersion and CLIL.

5.2 Minority Languages and Pedagogical Translanguaging

As we have seen in Section 3, pedagogical translanguaging is a pedagogic theory and practice integrating two or more languages, and often one or more of these languages can be a minority language. As Cenoz and Gorter (2017) explain, the situation of minority languages is dynamic and linked to social and political changes. Some regional minority languages have suffered oppression and have been excluded from the public domain for many years. However, some minority languages, such as Basque in Spain, Frisian in the Netherlands or Welsh in the United Kingdom, have received support in recent decades and are used as languages of instruction. For example, speakers of Basque as an L1 can now learn through the medium of this languages at school and at university and can be assessed in the minority language at all levels. The situation is quite different from that of Spanish or other minority-language speakers in the United States who need to develop 'academic English language and literacy' to succeed in 'college and careers' (García & Sylvan, 2011, p. 392). Basque L1 students are expected to develop academic language and literacy in the minority language as well as in Spanish, the majority language, because the aim is bilingualism (or trilingualism if English is also considered), but they can study and be assessed at all levels only in the minority language if that is their wish. Spontaneous translanguaging is common among students in the Basque Country whose L1 is Basque, but it is also common for these speakers to use Spanish, the majority language. The challenge is not to legitimise translanguaging but to stop these bilingual students (or their children in the future) from becoming monolingual Spanish speakers because Basque is no longer used. The social and historical context is quite different from that of Latinx students in the United States, where spontaneous translanguaging can empower language-minority students (García & Li, 2014). In the case of Basque or other regional minority languages such as Welsh, spontaneous translanguaging goes from the majority to the minority in that students tend to translanguage when they speak the minority language but not so much when they speak the majority language (Cenoz & Gorter, 2017). For example, Basque students hardly use features from the minority language when they use the majority language (Spanish), but spontaneous translanguaging in this context means that features from the majority language are used extensively when speaking the minority language. The social and historical context of regional minorities evidences the inequality between the languages, and there is considerable concern about the possible reinforcement of the majority language at the expense of the minority language if translanguaging is encouraged (Lewis, Jones & Baker, 2012b; Arocena, Cenoz, & Gorter; 2015; Gorter, 2015).

Students with majority languages as their L1 often learn through the minority language in regions where minority languages are spoken, such as Friesland, Brittany, Scotland, the Basque Country or Wales. This situation can be regarded as immersion or content-based instruction (CBI) because students who speak the majority language as the L1 are enrolled in programmes that have the L2 as the language of instruction for some or all the school subjects and have multilingualism as their aim (Cenoz, 2015). Students in these regions are often in the same class as students who speak Basque or Welsh as their L1. The relative number of students with one or the other language as their L1 will depend on the specific sociolinguistic context. Some students are early bilinguals with both the majority and minority languages as their first languages. Students with the majority language as their L1 are often exposed to the minority language only at school, and they use the majority language extensively. In this context, the question is not whether or not students translanguage but whether they use the majority language instead of the minority language.

Ballinger et al. (2017) consider that in the context of Canadian immersion, there is the risk that translanguaging practices will increase the use of English, the majority language, for most students. Even if French is not a minority language in other contexts, the only contact most students in French immersion have with French is at school. Using more English can have a negative effect on the use of French and also on the way students perceive the status of English as extremely powerful compared with the status of French (see also Lyster, 2019). Fortune and Tedick (2019) also highlight the importance of context in immersion programmes for speakers of English as an L1 in the United States as well as the risk of limiting exposure to the second language if the use of the majority language is encouraged (see also Cammarata & Tedick, 2012).

The risk of extending the use of the majority language usually refers to spontaneous translanguaging in these discussions. However, even when the use of resources from the whole linguistic repertoire is planned with a specific pedagogical purpose, pedagogical translanguaging could also pose a risk for the minority language. As Jones and Lewis (2014, 168) explain,

> [T]here is a growing concern that allowing the use of English texts for translanguaging purposes might be a stepping-stone for introducing more of the majority language (English). This is of particular concern to educators in areas where the minority language (Welsh) is already marginalized in the community outside the school.

Leonet, Cenoz and Gorter (2017) reported a general concern about Basque among teachers who had participated in a pedagogical translanguaging intervention but also considered that translanguaging pedagogies could be a rich experience for developing metalinguistic awareness. One of the teachers considered that having Basque along with more prestigious languages such as Spanish and English in the implementation of pedagogical translanguaging was positive for the prestige of Basque (Leonet, Cenoz and Gorter, 2017, p. 224). In spite of this positive comment, the potential of pedagogical translanguaging to change linguistic hierarchies raising the status of minority languages is limited (Lin, Wu & Lemke, 2020).

Ballinger et al. (2017, p. 36) show a preference for the term 'crosslinguistic pedagogy' instead of translanguaging or pedagogical translanguaging to refer to 'practices that support and encourage learners' drawing on their full linguistic repertoire in the classroom'. However, it is surprising to see that they refer to translanguaging in its original sense (Williams, 1996) not as translanguaging but as an example of crosslinguistic pedagogy. In this Element, we prefer to use the term 'pedagogical translanguaging' because it maintains the original term. Ballinger et al. (2017) consider that it can be a risk to encourage students to use features of the majority language in the time allocated to the minority language.

It is certainly true that the limited time devoted to the minority language should not be diminished, but pedagogical translanguaging practices go across the curriculum and the minority language can easily recover that time when it is used in the majority-language class as well. Using the minority language in the majority-language class not only implies a compensation of the amount of time, but it also raises both languages to the same level of prestige.

The concerns we have seen about the protection and development of minority languages in relation to pedagogical translanguaging show the need to consider the importance of context and the need to develop tailor-made programmes that ensure the development of the minority language. Cenoz and Gorter (2017) proposed some guiding principles for sustainable translanguaging for regional minority languages. One of these principles is to design functional breathing spaces for using the minority language. The concept of breathing space was mentioned by Fishman (1991, p. 59) and refers to a safe space (physical or otherwise) for the minority language, where it can 'breathe', enabling it to be used freely and without the threat of the majority language. The need for larger or smaller breathing spaces depends on the specific context in which the minority language is used. The need for spaces where only the minority language is used has been highlighted in different contexts (Cummins, 2007; García, 2009; Baker & Wright 2017).

Another guiding principle proposed by Cenoz and Gorter (2017) is the need to enhance language awareness. Taking into account the lower status of minority languages and immigrant languages as compared with majority languages, it is important that students discuss the social status and language practices of different languages in society (see also Melo-Pfeifer, 2015; Ganuza & Hedman, 2017; Duarte, 2020). Another principle guiding sustainable translanguaging is the development of metalinguistic awareness through pedagogical translanguaging practices that were referred to in Section 4. It is important that the situation is balanced so that pedagogical translanguaging is not restricted to the classes taught through the minority language but that elements of the minority language are also present in the classes taught in the majority language. Other guiding principles of sustainable translanguaging aim to create situations where the use of the minority language is needed and to build bridges between spontaneous and pedagogical translanguaging. One way to do this is to ask students to reflect on the way they translanguage in informal interactions and in pedagogical translanguaging activities so that they develop awareness about different contexts and uses of the minority languages (see also Section 4.2 for translanguaging shifts). In sum, it is possible to use pedagogical translanguaging in programmes aimed at maintaining and revitalising minority languages provided that minority languages have the space they need and full support.

5.3 Immersion, CLIL and Pedagogical Translanguaging

In this section, we look at pedagogical translanguaging as a pedagogy to face the challenges of learning content in a second or additional language in immersion and CLIL programmes. We consider that these programmes share the same core characteristics even if they tend to have differences in the number of subjects taught through the second or additional subject (Cenoz, Genesee & Gorter, 2014; Cenoz, 2015).

Immersion and CLIL programmes are challenging because academic content is learned through the medium of a second or additional language. Several studies have identified a language comprehension problem when subjects such as mathematics or science are taught in a second language (Roy, 2016; Clinton, Basaraba & Walkington, 2018; Prediger et al., 2018; Charamba, 2020). In the case of immersion and CLIL programmes, comprehension is challenging both for majority and minority L1 students (Lin, 2016; Mahan, 2020).

The language used in content subjects is in many cases substantially different from and more complex than the language used in English-language classes (Aguirregoitia Martinez, Bengoetxea Kortazar & Gonzalez-Dios, 2021). Many years ago, Cummins (1979) made a distinction between Cognitive/Academic Language Proficiency (CALP) and Basic Interpersonal Communicative Skills (BICS) to explain the difference between the type of proficiency needed to be successful at school and with everyday language. In fact, the comprehension and production of tasks require different levels of language that go beyond vocabulary and require the activation of prior knowledge and other complex skills. Uccelli et al. (2015) developed the construct Core Academic Language Skills (CALS) to define more precisely the linguistic features that are used in content areas across subjects (see also Barr, Uccelli & Phillips Galloway, 2019). CALS includes different domains such as unpacking, connecting ideas logically or tracking participants and themes, among others.

There are several strategies to help students to 'unpack academic language into everyday language as well as to repack everyday language into academic language' (Lin, 2016, p. 50). It is possible to build common experiences with students, to use visual representations and to ask students to write definitions using their own words (see Thompson et al., 2016). It is also possible to develop strategies based on pedagogical translanguaging.

As we have seen in Section 4, a strong form of pedagogical translanguaging involves using two or more languages so as to reflect on languages and develop metalinguistic awareness. In the case of immersion and CLIL, this strong form of pedagogical translanguaging can be applied to different linguistic forms and functions. For example, Arteagoitia and Howard (2015) reported the positive results of a pedagogical intervention using English-Spanish cognates (e.g. *incentive-incentivo*) so as to develop academic vocabulary and reading skills among Latinx students in the United States (see also García, Ibarra Johnson & Seltzer, 2017). English-Spanish cognates used in science and mathematics textbooks are very common, but there are also cognates among other languages (see Otwinowska, 2016, for Polish and English examples). Another way of developing metalinguistic awareness is by unpacking and packing complex words that have prefixes and suffixes by using prior knowledge in the whole linguistic repertoire (Lyster, Quiroga & Ballinger 2013; Leonet, Cenoz & Gorter, 2020).

Pedagogical translanguaging in immersion and CLIL programmes can also occur at the discourse level. The structure of texts and the linguistic resources used for different communicative functions when connecting ideas in a text can be compared in different languages (Cenoz & Gorter, 2020; Phillips Galloway, Uccelli & Aguilar, 2020). Pedagogical translanguaging can be helpful when using resources from the whole linguistic repertoire for reflecting on syntax, phonetics or pragmatics. So far we have looked at the strongest form of pedagogical translanguaging aimed at the development of metalinguistic awareness by comparing multilingual students' resources. Students have these resources, but pedagogical translanguaging seeks to activate them so that students can benefit from their own knowledge and achieve a better level of comprehension in the different disciplines taught though a second or additional language.

The use of two or more languages in the same class by comparing sources in different languages or changing the language for input and output can also be extremely useful in immersion and CLIL classes. This was proposed by Williams in Welsh and English in 1994, as we have seen in Section 2 (see Box 1). Cenoz and Santos (2020) also report an activity that is given in Section 4 as an example of the practice of enhancing metalinguistic awareness, in which students had to identify cognates; however, this activity is at the same time an example of the use of the whole linguistic repertoire because secondary school students also use four languages to listen, read and write some news items. The activities using input and output in different languages are close to the original use of the term 'translanguaging' in Wales but with a clear focus on metalinguistic awareness and applied to more languages. The original use of translanguaging in Wales and pedagogical translanguaging share the following crucial points: (i) the activities and the use of the languages are planned by the teacher and (ii) using more than one language can result in a deeper understanding of academic content (see also Baker, 2003; Lewis, Jones &

Baker, 2012a; Lin, 2016). Pedagogical translanguaging is a stronger form of translanguaging than just allowing for the use of the first language or other languages in immersion or CLIL programmes (see Section 2 and Nikula & Moore, 2016).

5.4 Summary

Translanguaging occurs in a wide variety of contexts, and special care is needed to protect and develop the use of minority languages so that translanguaging is sustainable. In some contexts, it is necessary to provide breathing spaces for the minority language and to guarantee that the time devoted to the minority language does not diminish as a result of translanguaging. Pedagogical translanguaging can be useful for facing the challenges of comprehension that majority and minority language students face in immersion and CLIL programmes.

6 Conclusion and Future Perspectives

By focusing on pedagogical translanguaging, this Element goes against long-standing traditions of language separation when teaching languages and academic content in school contexts. Kramsch (2012, p. 109) considers that adopting multilingual perspectives such as pedagogical translanguaging is revolutionary because 'it puts into question the whole monolingual foundation of theoretical and applied linguistics'.

Pedagogical translanguaging is at the crossroads of several areas of applied linguistics because it is related to bilingual and multilingual education, second and foreign language acquisition and teaching and majority and minority languages. It is rooted in the original concept of 'translanguaging' in Welsh bilingual education, which aims at developing language and academic skills by implementing activities using two languages in the same lesson (Williams, 1994). Pedagogical translanguaging broadens the original concept by including a wide range of possibilities beyond the alternation of languages in the input and output and also by proposing the integrated use of languages for phonetic, lexical, morphosyntactic, pragmatic and discourse levels. Moreover, pedagogical translanguaging is not limited to two languages and can include three or more.

Pedagogical translanguaging aims to develop multilingualism across the curriculum. A key feature is that it activates prior knowledge, which in this context refers to the pre-existing knowledge that students have in their multilingual repertoire (see our video *Let's Make the Most of Multilingualism*, Cenoz & Gorter, 2018). A key feature is that it activates prior knowledge, which in this context refers to the pre-existing knowledge that students have in their multilingual repertoire. By activating this knowledge, students make more progress in the development of their multilingual competence. Pedagogical translanguaging adopts a heteroglossic multilingual approach to enhance linguistic and academic development through the implementation of planned didactic activities. Another key feature of pedagogical translanguaging is metalinguistic awareness, understood as the ability to reflect on language and to focus on language as an object (Jessner, 2006). Pedagogical translanguaging practices can have different levels of intensity. The strongest practices aim at enhancing metalinguistic awareness by analysing and reflecting on language when using two or more languages for teaching in the same lesson. The focus on metalinguistic awareness is not as strong in other pedagogical translanguaging practices as we have seen in Section 4.

This Element also considers multilingual assessment as an integral part of education. As we have also seen in Section 4, exams and tests in more than one language can be used to make sure that students understand their tasks (see for example Heugh et al., 2017). Another perspective is to simultaneously assess performance in two or more languages side by side instead of independently (Cenoz, Arocena & Gorter, 2013; Escamilla et al., 2013). In this way, the global assessment of multilingual competence can be seen while the strengths and weaknesses of students in the different languages can also be identified. Some progress has been made in multilingual assessment, but there is still much left to be done.

Pedagogical translanguaging can enhance the comprehension of academic content at different levels. The resources multilingual students have in their whole linguistic repertoire can be useful to reflect crosslinguistically when unpacking complex vocabulary, analysing the structure of a text or understanding logical connectors.

A key idea in this Element is context. Pedagogical translanguaging has to be designed and implemented taking into account the characteristics of the school context and the sociolinguistic context where the school is located. The school context refers to the aims of the programme, the language(s) of the students and teachers, the languages in the curriculum and the languages of communication at school (see also Leung & Valdés, 2019). The sociolinguistic context refers to the languages used in the specific community where the school is located and the institutional support these languages receive. In the wider context, the national and international prestige of the languages involved is also important. In this Element, we highlight that pedagogical translanguaging has to be sustainable so as to promote the protection and development of minority languages.

To summarise, as a theoretical and practical approach, pedagogical translanguaging aims at improving learning across the curriculum. In this Element, we present its core characteristics and propose practices that can maximise the resources multilingual students have at their disposal.

Future progress in this area will depend on the development of theoretical and empirical studies that can take the state-of-the-art on pedagogical translanguaging further. A pressing challenge, among others, is to obtain evidence regarding the optimal ages, grades, intensity and the required level of multilingual competence for its implementation, as well as the specific ways to make translanguaging sustainable in the case of minority languages. The number of studies comparing the results obtained in language and content by groups that have followed translanguaging pedagogies and control groups is still very limited, and it is necessary to confirm the positive findings in different contexts.

In fact, languages can be regarded as friends and not enemies. Schools have traditionally adopted monolingual ideologies and have tried to isolate languages, but multilingual speakers' languages are not isolated. Speakers know that depending on their interlocutors, they can use one of their languages in some contexts, while in others they can use resources from their whole linguistic repertoire so as to communicate more effectively. The number of languages taught at school and the number of different home languages are increasing in many contexts, but multilingual practices have a long historical tradition. The Behistun Inscription in the Old Persian, Elamite and Babylonian languages or the Rosetta Stone in Ancient Egyptian hieroglyphs, Demotic script and Greek are examples showing that languages were written side by side many centuries ago.

Pedagogical translanguaging aims at helping students learn languages and academic content more efficiently. Dr. Elka Todeva (2009, p. 57), an accomplished polyglot with a high level of metalinguistic awareness, explained that when learning Spanish and Italian, her knowledge of other languages was very helpful: 'As a multilingual, I was getting many such "free rides" and was empowered significantly.'

Pedagogical translanguaging aims to empower multilingual students who have not reached this point and need to develop their metalinguistic awareness crosslinguistically so as to benefit from their own multilingual repertoire. Improved multilingual competence will certainly lead to the acquisition of additional languages and a deeper understanding of academic subjects.

References

Aguirregoitia Martinez, A., Bengoetxea Kortazar, K. & Gonzalez-Dios, I. (2021). Are CLIL texts too complicated? A computational analysis of their linguistic characteristics. *Journal of Immersion and Content-Based Language Education*, 9, 4–30. doi: 10.1075/jicb.19022.agu

Angelovska, T. (2018). Cross-linguistic awareness of adult L3 learners of English: A focus on metalinguistic reflections and proficiency. *Language Awareness*, 27, 136–52. doi: 10.1080/09658416.2018.1431243

Angelovska, T. & Hahn, A. (2014). Raising language awareness for learning and teaching grammar. In A. Benati, C. Laval & M. Arche, eds., *The Grammar Dimension in Instructed Second Language Learning*. London: Bloomsbury Academic, pp. 185–207.

Apraiz Jaio, M. V., Pérez Gómez, M. & Ruiz Pérez, T. (2012). La enseñanza integrada de las lenguas in la escuela plurilingüe. *Revista Iberoamericana de Educación*, 59, 119–37. doi: 10.35362/rie590459

Arocena, E., Cenoz, J. & Gorter, D. (2015). Teachers' beliefs in multilingual education in the Basque Country and in Friesland. *Journal of Immersion and Content-Based Language Education*, 3, 169–93. doi:10.1075/jicb.3.2.01aro

Arteagoitia, I. & Howard, L. (2015). The role of the native language in the literacy development of Latino students in the U.S. In J. Cenoz & D. Gorter, eds., *Multilingual Education: Between Language Learning and Translanguaging*. Cambridge: Cambridge University Press, pp. 61–83.

Baker, C. (2000). *The Care and Education of Young Bilinguals*. Clevedon, UK: Multilingual Matters.

Baker, C. (2003). Biliteracy and transliteracy in Wales: Language planning and the Welsh national curriculum. In N. Hornberger, ed., *Continua of Biliteracy*. Clevedon, UK: Multilingual Matters, pp. 71–90.

Baker, C. & Wright, W. E. (2017). *Foundations of Bilingual Education and Bilingualism*. Bristol, UK: Multilingual Matters.

Ballinger, S., Lyster, R., Sterzuk, A. & Genesee, F. (2017). Context-appropriate crosslinguistic pedagogy: Considering the role of language status in immersion education. *Journal of Immersion and Content-Based Language Education*, 5, 30–57. doi: 10.1075/jicb.5.1.02bal

Barr, C. D., Uccelli, P. & Phillips Galloway, E. (2019). Specifying the academic language skills that support text understanding in the middle grades: The design and validation of the core academic language skills construct and instrument. *Language Learning*, 69, 978–1021. doi: 10.1111/lang.12365

Bialystok, E. & Barac, R. (2012). Emerging bilingualism: Dissociating advantages for metalinguistic awareness and executive control. *Cognition*, 122, 67–73. doi: 10.1016/j.cognition.2011.08.003

Block, D. (2007). Bilingualism: Four assumptions and four responses. *Innovation in Language Learning and Teaching*, 1, 66–82. doi: 10.2167/illt043.0

Bransford, J. D., Brown, A. L. & Cocking, R. R., Eds (2000). *How People Learn: Brain, Mind Experience and School*. Washington, DC: National Academies Press.

Cammarata, L. & Tedick, D. (2012). Balancing content and language in instruction: The experience of immersion teachers. *The Modern Language Journal*, 96, 251–269. doi:10.1111/j.1540-4781. 2012.01330.x

Canagarajah, S. (2007). Lingua franca English, multilingual communities, and language acquisition. *Modern Language Journal*, 91, 921–37. doi:10.1111/j.1540-4781.2007.00678.x

Canagarajah,S. (2013). *Translingual Practice: Global Englishes and Cosmopolitan Relations*. New York: Routledge.

Canagarajah, S. (2018). Translingual practice as spatial repertoires: Expanding the paradigm beyond structuralist orientations. *Applied Linguistics*, 39, 31–54. doi: 10.1093/applin/amx041

Cenoz, J. (2003). The additive effect of bilingualism on third language acquisition: A review. *The International Journal of Bilingualism* 7, 71–88. doi: 10.1177/13670069030070010501

Cenoz, J. (2009). *Towards Multilingual Education*. Bristol, UK: Multilingual Matters.

Cenoz, J. (2013). The influence of bilingualism on third language acquisition: Focus on multilingualism. *Language Teaching*, 46, 71–86. doi: 10.1017/S0261444811000218

Cenoz, J. (2015). Content-based instruction and content and language integrated learning: The same or different? *Language, Culture and Curriculum*, 28, 8–24. doi: 10.1080/07908318.2014.1000922

Cenoz, J. (2017). Translanguaging in school context. International perspectives: An introduction. *Journal of Language, Identity and Education*, 16, 193–1-98. doi: 10.1080/15348458.2017.1327816

Cenoz, J., Arocena, E. & Gorter, D. (2013). Multilingual students and their writing skills in Basque, Spanish and English. In V. Mueller Gathercole, ed., *Issues in the Assessment of Bilinguals*. Bristol UK: Multilingual Matters, pp. 186–205.

Cenoz, J. & Bereziartua, G. (2016). Is Instant Messaging the same in every language? A Basque perspective. *Reading and Writing*, 29, 1225–1243. doi:10.1007/s11145-016-9634-z

Cenoz, J., Genesee, F. & Gorter, D. (2014). Critical analysis of CLIL: Taking stock and looking forward. *Applied Linguistics*, 35, 243–62. doi: 10.1093/applin/amt011

Cenoz, J. & Gorter, D. (2011). Focus on multilingualism: A study of trilingual writing. *The Modern Language Journal*, 95, 356–69. doi: 10.1111/j.1540-4781.2011.01206.x

Cenoz, J. & Gorter, D. (2013). Towards a plurilingual approach in English language teaching: Softening the boundaries between languages. *TESOL Quaterly*, 47, 591–599. doi: 10.1002/tesq.121

Cenoz, J. & Gorter, D. (2014). Focus on multilingualism as an approach in educational contexts. In A. Creese & A. Blackledge, eds., *Heteroglossia as Practice and Pedagogy*. Berlin: Springer, pp. 239–54.

Cenoz, J. & Gorter, D. (2015). Towards a holistic approach in the study of multilingual education. In J. Cenoz & D. Gorter, eds., *Multilingual Education: Between Language Learning and Translanguaging*. Cambridge: Cambridge University Press, pp. 1–15.

Cenoz, J. & Gorter, D. (2017). Sustainable translanguaging and minority languages: Threat or opportunity? *Journal of Multilingual and Multicultural Development*, 38, 901–12. doi: 10.1080/01434632.2017.1284855

Cenoz, J. & Gorter, D. (2018). Let's make the most of multilingualism. Online video clip. www.youtube.com/watch?v=vg8i2UHAf8s

Cenoz, J. & Gorter, D. (2020). Pedagogical translanguaging: An introduction. *System*, 92. doi: 10.1016/j.system.2020.102269

Cenoz, J. & Santos, A. (2020). Implementing pedagogical translanguaging in trilingual schools. *System*, 92. doi: 10.1016/j.system.2020.102273

Charamba, E. (2020). Translanguaging: Developing scientific scholarship in a multilingual classroom. *Journal of Multilingual and Multicultural Development*, 41, 655–72. doi: 10.1080/01434632.2019.1625907

Clinton, V., Basaraba, D. L. & Walkington, C. (2018). English learners and mathematical word problem solving: A systematic review. In D. L. Baker, D. L. Basaraba & C. Richards-Tutor, eds., *Second Language Acquisition: Methods, Perspectives and Challenges*. New York: Nova Science, pp. 171–208.

Cook, V. (1992). Evidence for multi-competence. *Language Learning*, 42, 557–91. doi: 10.1111/j.1467-1770.1992.tb01044.x

Cook V. (2010). The relationship between first and second language acquisition revisited. In E. Macaro, ed., *The Continuum Companion to Second Language Acquisition*. London: Continuum, pp. 137–57.

Cook, V. & Bassetti, B. (2005). An introduction to researching second language writing systems. In V. Cook & B. Bassetti, eds, *Second Language Writing Systems*. Clevedon, UK: Multilingual Matters, pp. 1–70.

Council of Europe. (2001). *Common European Framework of Reference for Languages*. Cambridge: Cambridge University Press. https://rm.coe.int /1680459f97

Council of Europe. (2011). *The European Language Portfolio*. www.coe.int/en/ web/portfolio

Council of Europe. (2018). *Common European Framework of Reference for Languages: Learning, Teaching, Assessment. Companion Volume with New Descriptors*. https://rm.coe.int/cefr-companion-volume-with-new-descrip tors-2018/1680787989

Creese, A. & Blackledge, A. (2010). Translanguaging in the bilingual class-room: A pedagogy for learning and teaching? *The Modern Language Journal*, 94, 103–15. doi: 10.1111/j.1540-4781.2009.00986.x

Cummins, J. (1979). Cognitive/academic language proficiency, linguistic inter-dependence, the optimum age question and some other matters. *Working Papers on Bilingualism*, 19, 121–129.

Cummins, J. (2007). Rethinking monolingual instructional strategies in multi-lingual classrooms. *Canadian Journal of Applied Linguistics* 10, 221–40. https://journals.lib.unb.ca/index.php/CJAL/article/view/19743

Cummins, J. (2017). Teaching for transfer in multilingual school contexts. In O. García, A. Lin & S. May, eds., *Bilingual Education: Encyclopedia of Language and Education*, Vol. 5. Berlin: Springer, pp. 103–15.

Cummins, J. (2021a). Translanguaging: A critical analysis of theoretical claims. In P. Juvonen & M. Källkvist, eds, *Pedagogical Translanguaging: Theoretical, Methodological and Empirical Perspectives*. Bristol, UK: UK Multilingual Matters

Cummins, J. (2021b). *Rethinking the Education of Multilingual Learners*. Bristol, UK: Multilingual Matters.

Daniel, S., Jiménez, R. T., Pray, L. & Pacheco, M. B. (2019). Scaffolding to make translanguaging a classroom norm. *TESOL Journal*, 10, 1–14. doi:10.1002/tesj.361

De Angelis, G. (2007). *Third or Additional Language Learning*. Clevedon,UK: Multilingual Matters.

De Backer, F., Slembrouck, S. & Van Avermaet, P. (2019). Assessment accom-modations for multilingual learners: Pupils' perceptions of fairness. *Journal of Multilingual and Multicultural Development*, 40, 833–46. doi: 10.1080/ 01434632.2019.1571596

De Backer, F., Van Avermaet, P. & Slembrouck, S. (2017). Schools as labora-tories for exploring multilingual assessment policies and practices. *Language and Education*, 31, 217–30. doi:10.1080/09500782.2016 .1261896

De Bot, K., Lowie, W. M. & Verspoor, M. H. (2007). A dynamic systems theory approach to second language acquisition. *Bilingualism: Language and Cognition*, 10, 7–21. doi: 10.1017/S1366728906002732

Douglas Fir Group. (2016). A transdisciplinary framework for SLA in a multilingual world. *The Modern Language Journal*, 100, 19–47. doi: 10.1111/modl.12301

Duarte, J. (2020). Translanguaging in the context of mainstream multilingual education. *International Journal of Multilingualism*, 17, 232–47. doi: 10.1080/14790718.2018.1512607

Duarte, J. & Kirsch, C. (2020). Introduction: multilingual approaches to teaching and learning. In C. Kirsch & J. Duarte, eds., *Multilingual Approaches for Teaching and Learning. From Acknowledging to Capitalising on Multilingualism in European Mainstream Education*. New York: Routledge, pp. 1–12.

Escamilla, K., Hopewell, S., Butvilofsky, S., Sparrow, W., Soltero-Gonzalez, L., Ruiz-Figueroa, O. & Escamilla, M. (2013). *Biliteracy from the Start: Literacy Squared in Action*. Philadelphia, PA: Caslon.

Falk, Y., Lindqvist, C. & Bardel, C. (2015). The role of L1 explicit metalinguistic knowledge in L3 oral production at the initial state. *Bilingualism: Language and Cognition* 18: 227–35. doi: 10.1017/S1366728913000552

Fishman, J. A. (1991). *Reversing Language Shift: Theoretical and Empirical Foundations of Assistance to Threatened Languages*. Philadelphia, PA: Multilingual Matters.

Fortune, T. W. & Tedick, D. J. (2019). Context matters: Translanguaging and language immersion education in the US and Canada. In M. Haneda & H. Nassaji, eds., *Perspectives on Language as Action: Festschrift in Honour of Merrill Swain*. Bristol, UK: Multilingual Matters, pp. 27–44.

Gabrys-Barker, D. (2012). *Cross-linguistic Influences in Multilingual Language Acquisition*. Berlin: Springer.

Galante, A. (2020a). Translanguaging for vocabulary development: A mixed methods study with international students in a Canadian English for Academic Purposes program. In Z. Tian, L. Aghai, P. Sayer & J. L. Schissel, eds., *Envisioning TESOL Through a Translanguaging Lens*. Cham, Denmark: Springer, pp. 293–328.

Galante, A. (2020b). Pedagogical translanguaging in a multilingual English program in Canada: Student and teacher perspectives of challenges. *System* 92, 1–16. doi: 10.1016/j.system.2020.102274

Ganuza, N. & Hedman, C. (2017). Ideology vs. practice: Is there a space for translanguaging in mother tongue instruction? In B. A. Paulsrud, J. Rosén,

B. Straszer & A. Wedin, eds., *New Perspectives on Translanguaging and Education*. Bristol, UK: Multilingual Matters, pp. 208–26.

García, O. (2009). *Bilingual Education in the 21st Century: A Global Perspective*. Malden/Oxford: Wiley/Blackwell.

García, O., Ibarra Johnson, S. & Seltzer, K. (2017). *The Translanguaging Classroom*. Philadelphia, PA: Caslon.

García, O. & Li, W. (2014). *Translanguaging: Language, Bilingualism and Education*. London: Palgrave Macmillan.

García, O. & Lin, A. (2017). Translanguaging and bilingual education. In O. García, A. Lin, & S. May, eds., *Bilingual Education: Encyclopedia of Language and Education*, Vol. 5. Berlin: Springer, pp. 117 –30.

García, O. & Otheguy, R. (2020). Plurilingualism and translanguaging: Commonalities and divergences. *International Journal of Bilingual Education and Bilingualism*, 23, 17–35. doi: 10.1080/13670050.2019.1598932

García, O. & Sylvan, C. E. (2011). Pedagogies and practices in multilingual classrooms: Singularities in pluralities. *The Modern Language Journal*, 95, 385–400. doi: 10.1111/j.1540-4781.2011.01208.x

Gollub, J. P., Berthanthal, M., Labov, J. & Curtis, C., eds, (2002). *Learning and Understanding: Improving Advanced Study of Mathematics and Science in U.S. High Schools*. Washington, DC: National Academies Press.

Gorter, D. (2015). Multilingual interaction and minority languages: Proficiency and language practices in education and society. *Language Teaching*, 48, 82–98. doi: 10.1017/S0261444812000481

Gorter, D. & Cenoz, J. (2017). Language education policy and multilingual assessment. *Language and Education* 31, 231–48. doi: 10.1080/09500782.2016.1261892

Gorter, D., Zenotz, V. & Cenoz, J.. eds., (2014). *Minority Languages and Multilingual Education: Bridging the Local and the Global*. Berlin: Springer.

Herdina, P. & Jessner, U. (2002). *A Dynamic Model of Multilingualism: Changing the Psycholinguistic Perspective*. Clevedon,UK: Multilingual Matters.

Heugh, K., Prinsloo, C., Makgamatha, M., Diedericks, G. & Winnaar, L. (2017). Multilingualism(s) and system-wide assessment: A southern perspective. *Language and Education*, 31, 197–216. doi: 10.1080/09500782.2016.1261894

Hofer, B. & Jessner, U. (2019). Assessing components of multi-(lingual) competence in young learners. *Lingua* 19, 232. doi: 10.1016/j.lingua.2019.102747

Huang, K. J. (2018). On bilinguals' development of metalinguistic awareness and its transfer to L3 learning: The role of language characteristics.

International Journal of Bilingualism, 22, 330–3-49. doi: 10.1177/1367006916681081

Izadi, M. & Yarahmadzehi, N. (2020). The metalinguistic awareness of bilingual (Persian-Baluchi) and monolingual (Persian) learners of English language. *Linguistic Approaches to Bilingualism*, 10, 249–89. doi: 10.1075/lab.16012.iza

Jacobs, H. L., Zingraf, S. A., Wormuth, D. R., Hartfiel, V. F. & Hughey, J. B. (1981). *Testing ESL composition*. Rowley, MA: Newbury House.

Jacobson, R. (1990). Allocating two languages as a key feature of a bilingual methodology. In R. Jacobson & C. Faltis, eds., *Language Distribution Issues in Bilingual Schooling*. Clevedon, UK: Multilingual Matters, pp. 3–17.

Jarvis, S. & Pavlenko, A. (2008). *Crosslinguistic Influence in Language and Cognition*. New York: Routledge.

Jaspers, J. (2018). The transformative limits of translanguaging. *Language & Communication*, 58, 1–10. doi: 10.1016/j.langcom.2017.12.001

Jessner, U. (2006). *Linguistic Awareness in Multilinguals: English as a Third Language*. Edinburgh: Edinburgh University Press.

Jessner, U. (2008). Teaching third languages: Findings, trends, and challenges. *Language Teaching*, 41, 15–56.

Jones, B. & Lewis W. G. (2014). Language arrangements within bilingual education in Wales. In E. M. Thomas & I. Mennen, eds., *Advances in the Study of Bilingualism*. Bristol, UK: Multilingual Matters, pp. 141–70.

Kostons, D. & van der Werf, G. (2015). The effects of activating prior topic and metacognitive knowledge on text comprehension scores. *British Journal of Educational Psychology*, 85, 264–75. doi: 10.1111/bjep.12069

Kramsch, C. (2010). *The Multilingual Subject*. Oxford: Oxford University Press.

Kramsch, C. (2012). Authenticity and legitimacy in multilingual SLA. *Critical Multilingualism Studies*, 1, 107–28.

Kupers, E., van Dijk, M. & van Geert, P. (2017). Changing patterns of scaffolding and autonomy during individual music lessons: A mixed methods approach. *Journal of the Learning Sciences*, 26, 131–66. doi: 10.1080/10508406.2016.1259624

Larsen-Freeman, D. (2007). On the complementarity of chaos/complexity theory and dynamic systems theory in understanding the second language acquisition process. *Bilingualism: Language and Cognition*, 10, 35–7.

Lasagabaster, D. (1998). Metalinguistic awareness and the learning of English as an L3. *Atlantis*, 20, 69–79.

Leonet, O. ; Cenoz, J. & Gorter, D. (2017). Challenging minority language isolation: Translanguaging in a trilingual school in the Basque Country.

Journal of Language, Identity and Education, 16, 216–27. doi: 10.1080/ 15348458.2017.1328281

Leonet, O. ; Cenoz, J. & Gorter, D. (2020). Developing morphological awareness across languages: Translanguaging pedagogies in third language acquisition. *Language Awareness*, 29, 41–59. doi: 10.1080/ 09658416.2019.1688338

Leow, R. P. (1997). Attention, awareness, and foreign language behavior. *Language Learning*, 47, 467–505.

Leung, C. & Valdés, G. (2019). Translanguaging and the transdisciplinary framework for language teaching and learning in a multilingual world. *Modern Language Journal*, 103, 348–70. doi: 10.1111/modl.12568

Lewis, G., Jones, B. & Baker, C. (2012a). Translanguaging: Origins and development from school to street and beyond. *Educational Research and Evaluation*, 18, 641–54. doi: 10.1080/13803611.2012.718488

Lewis, G., Jones, B. & Baker, C. (2012b). Translanguaging: Developing its conceptualisation and contextualization. *Educational Research and Evaluation*, 18, 655–70. doi: 10.1080/13803611.2012.718490

Li, W. (2011). Moment analysis and translanguaging space: Discursive construction of identities by multilingual Chinese youth in Britain. *Journal of Pragmatics*, 43, 1222–35. doi: 10.1016/j.pragma.2010.07.035

Li, W. (2018). Translanguaging as a practical theory of language. *Applied Linguistics*, 39, 9–30. doi: 10.1093/applin/amx039

Lin, A. M. Y. (2016). *Language Across the Curriculum & CLIL in English as an Additional Language (EAL) Contexts: Theory and Practice.* Singapore: Springer.

Lin A. M.Y. (2020). Introduction: Translanguaging and translanguaging pedagogies. In V. Vaish, ed., *Translanguaging in Multilingual English Classrooms.* Berlin: Springer, pp. 1–9.

Lin, A. M. Y. & Lo, Y. Y. (2016). Trans/languaging and the triadic dialogue in Content and Language Integrated Learning (CLIL) classrooms. *Language and Education*, 31, 1–20. doi: 10.1080/09500782.2016.1230125

Lin, A. M. Y., Wu, Y., & Lemke, J. L. (2020). 'It takes a village to research a village': Conversations between Angel Lin and Jay Lemke on contemporary issues in translanguaging. In S. M. C. Lau & S. Van Viegen, eds., *Plurilingual Pedagogies: Critical and Creative Endeavors for Equitable Language in Education.* Cham, Denmark: Springer, pp. 47–74.

Llurda, E. (2014).*Native and non-native teachers of English.* In C. Chapelle, ed., *The Encyclopedia of Applied Linguistics.* London: Wiley, 1–5.

Lyster, R. (2019). Translanguaging in immersion: Cognitive support or social prestige? *The Canadian Modern Language Review*, 75, 340–52. doi: 10.3138/cmlr.2019-0038

Lyster, R., Collins, L. & Ballinger, S. (2009). Linking languages through a bilingual read-aloud project. *Language Awareness*, 18, 366–83. doi: 10.1080/09658410903197322

Lyster, R., Quiroga, J. & Ballinger, S. (2013). The effects of biliteracy instruction on morphological awareness. *Journal of Immersion and Content-Based Language Education*, 1, 169–97. doi: 10.1075/jicb.1.2.02lys

MacSwan, J. (2017). A multilingual perspective on translanguaging. *American Educational Research Journal*, 54, 167–201. doi: 10.3102/0002831216683935

Mahan, K. R. (2020). The comprehending teacher: Scaffolding in content and language integrated learning (CLIL), *The Language Learning Journal*. doi: 10.1080/09571736.2019.1705879

Makoni, S. & Pennycook, A. D. (2007). Disinventing and reconstituting languages. In S. Makoni & A. Pennycook, eds., *Disinventing and Reconstituting Languages*. Clevedon, UK: Multilingual Matters, pp. 1–41.

Melo-Pfeifer, S. (2015). Multilingual awareness and heritage language education: Children's multimodal representations of their multilingualism. *Language Awareness*, 24, 197–215. doi: 10.1080/09658416.2015.1072208

Menken, K. & Sánchez, M. (2019). Translanguaging in English-only schools: From pedagogy to stance in the disruption of monolingual policies and practices. *TESOL Quarterly*. 53, 741–67. doi: 10.1002/tesq.513

Montrul, S. & Silva-Corvalán, C. (2019). The social context contributes to the incomplete acquisition of aspects of heritage languages. *Studies in Second Language Acquisition*, 41, 269–73. doi: 10.1017/S0272263119000354

Morales, J. Schissel, J. L. & López-Gopar, M. (2020). Pedagogical sismo: Translanguaging approaches for English language instruction and assessment in Oaxaca, Mexico. In Z. Tian, L. Aghai, P. Sayer & J. L. Schissel, eds., *Envisioning TESOL through a Translanguaging Lens: Global Perspectives*. Cham, Denmark: Springer International, pp. 161–83.

Nikula, T., & Moore, P. (2016). Exploring translanguaging in CLIL. *International Journal of Bilingual Education and Bilingualism*, 19, 1–13. doi: 10.1080/13670050.2016.1254151

Ortega, L. (2019). SLA and the study of equitable multilingualism. *Modern Language Journal*, 103, 23–38. doi: 10.1111/modl.12525

Otheguy, R. (2016). The linguistic competence of second-generation bilinguals: A critique of 'incomplete acquisition'. In C. Tortora, M. den Dikken, I. L. Montoya & T. O'Neill, eds., *Romance Linguistics*. Amsterdam: John Benjamins, pp. 301–20.

Otheguy, R., García, O., & Reid, W. (2015). Clarifying translanguaging and deconstructing named languages: A perspective from linguistics. *Applied Linguistics Review*, 6, 281–307. doi: 10.1515/applirev-2015-0014

Otheguy, R., García, O. & Reid, W. (2019). A translanguaging view of the linguistic system of bilinguals. *Applied Linguistics Review*, 10: 625–51. doi: 10.1515/applirev-2018-0020

Otwinowska, A. (2016). *Cognate Vocabulary in Language Acquisition and Use: Attitudes, Awareness, Activation*. Bristol, UK: Multilingual Matters.

Phillips Galloway, E., Uccelli, P., Aguilar, G. & Barr, C. D. (2020). Exploring the crosslinguistic contribution of Spanish and English academic language skills to English text comprehension for middle-grade dual language learners. *AERA Open*, 6. doi: 10.1177/2332858419892575

Poza, L. (2017). Translanguaging: Definitions, implications, and further needs in burgeoning inquiry. *Berkeley Review of Education*, 6, 101–28.

Prediger, S., Wilhelm, N., Büchter, A., Gürsoy, E. & Benholz, C. (2018). Language proficiency and mathematics achievement – Empirical study of language-induced obstacles in a high stakes test, the central exam ZP10. *Journal für Mathematik-Didaktik*, 39 (Supp. 1), 1–26. doi: 10.1007/s13138-018-0126-3

Rauch, D., Naumann, J. & Jude, N. (2011). Metalinguistic awareness mediates effects of full biliteracy on third-language reading proficiency in Turkish–German bilinguals. *International Journal of Bilingualism*, 16, 402–18. doi: 10.1177%2F1367006911425819

Roy, S. (2016). Assessing bilingual and multilingual learners in mainstream classrooms. In S. Scott, D. E. Scott & C. F. Webber, eds., *Leadership of Assessment, Inclusion, and Learning*. Princeton, NJ: Springer, pp. 225–41.

Rutgers, R. & Evans, M. (2017). Bilingual education and L3 learning: Metalinguistic advantage or not? *International Journal of Bilingual Education and Bilingualism*, 20(7), 788–806. doi:10.1080/13670050.2015.1103698

Santos, A., Cenoz, J. & Gorter, D. (2017). Communicative anxiety in English as a third language. *International Journal of Bilingual Education and Bilingualism*, 20, 823–36. doi: 10.1080/13670050.2015.1105780

Schissel, J. L., Leung, C. & Chalhoub-Deville, M. (2019). The construct of multilingualism in language testing. *Language Assessment Quarterly*, 16(4–5), 373–8. doi: 10.1080/15434303.2019.1680679

Schissel, J. L., Leung, C., López-Gopar, M. E. & Davis, J. R. (2018). Multilingual learners in language assessment: Assessment design for linguistically diverse communities. *Language and Education*, 32, 167–82. doi:10.1080/09500782.2018.1429463

Shohamy, E. (2011). Assessing multilingual competencies: Adopting construct valid assessment policies. *The Modern Language Journal* 95, 418–29. doi:10.1111/j.1540-4781.2011.01210.x.

Shohamy, E. & Menken, K. (2015). Language assessment: Past to present misuses and future possibilities. In W. . Wright, S. Boun & O. García, eds., *Handbook of Bilingual and Multilingual Education*, Hoboken, NJ: Wiley-Blackwell, pp. 253–69.

Slembrouck, S. & Rosiers, K. (2018). Translanguaging: A matter of sociolinguistics, pedagogics and interaction? In P. Van Avermaet, S. Slembrouck, K. Van Gorp, S. Sierens & K. Maryns, eds., *The Multilingual Edge of Education*. London: Palgrave Macmillan, pp. 165–87.

Slembrouck, S., Van Avermaet, P. & Van Gorp, K. (2018). Strategies of ultilingualism in education for minority children. In P. Van Avermaet, S. Slembrouck, K. Van Gorp, S. Sierens & K. Maryns, eds., *The Multilingual Edge of Education*. London: Palgrave Macmillan, pp. 9–39.

Spoelman, M. & Verspoor, M. (2010). Dynamic patterns in development of accuracy and complexity: A longitudinal case study in the acquisition of Finnish. *Applied Linguistics*, 31, 532–53. doi: 10.1093/applin/amq001

Swain, M. & Lapkin, S. (2013). A Vygotskian sociocultural perspective on immersion education: The L1/L2 debate. *Journal of Immersion and Content-Based Language Education*, 1, 101–30. doi: 10.1075/jicb.1.1.05swa

Swain, M., & Suzuki, W. (2008). Interaction, output, and communicative language learning. In B. Spolsky & F. M. Hult, eds., *The Handbook of Educational Linguistics*. Oxford: Blackwell, pp. 557–68.

Tedick, D., & Lyster. R. (2020). *Scaffolding Language Development in Immersion and Dual Language Classrooms*. New York: Routledge.

Todeva, E. (2009). Multilingualism as a kaleidoscopic experience: The mini-universes within. In E. Todeva & J. Cenoz, eds., *The Multiple Realities of Multingualism: Personal Narratives and Researchers' Perspectives*. Berlin and New York: Mouton De Gruyter, pp. 53–74.

Thomas, J. (1988). The role played by metalinguistic awareness in second- and third-language learning. *Journal of Multilingual and Multicultural Development*, 9, 235–46. doi: 10.1080/01434632.1988.9994334

Thompson, D. R., Kersaint, G., Vorster, H., Webb, L., & Van der Walt, M. S. (2016). Addressing multi-language diversity in mathematics teacher education programs. In R. Barwell, P. Clarkson, A. Halai, M. Kazima, J. Moschkovich, N. Planas, M. Setati-Phakeng, P. Valero & M. V. Ubillús, eds., *Mathematics Education and Language Diversity: The 21st ICMI Study*. Berlin: Springer, pp. 121–39.

Uccelli, P., Barr, C. D., Dobbs, C. L., Phillips Galloway, E., Meneses, A. & Sánchez, E. (2015). Core academic language skills (CALS): An expanded operational construct and a novel instrument to chart school-relevant language proficiency in pre-adolescent and adolescent learners. *Applied Psycholinguistics*, 36, 1077–109. doi:10.1017/S014271641400006X

Vaish, V. (2020). *Translanguaging in Multilingual English Classrooms*. Berlin: Springer.

Van den Broek, P., White, M. J., Kendeou, P. & Carlson, S. (2009). Reading between the lines: Developmental and individual differences in cognitive processes in reading comprehension. In R. K. Wagner, C. Schatschneider & C. Phythian-Sence, eds., *Beyond Decoding: The Behavioral and Biological Foundations of Reading Comprehension*. New York: Guilford, pp. 107–23.

Van Geert, P. (1994). *Dynamic Systems of Development: Change between Complexity and Chaos*.Hertfordshire, UK: Harvester Wheatsheaf.

Van Geert, P. (2003). Dynamic systems approaches and modeling of developmental processes. In J. Valsiner & K. J. Connolly, eds., *Handbook of Developmental Psychology*. London: Sage, pp. 640–72.

Van Geert, P., & Steenbeek, H. (2005). The dynamics of scaffolding. *New Ideas in Psychology*, 23, 115–28. doi: 10.1016/j.newideapsych.2006.05.003

Verspoor, M., Lowie, W. & van Dijk, M. (2008). Variability in L2 development from a dynamic systems perspective. *The Modern Language Journal*, 92, 214–31. doi: 10.1111/j.1540-4781.2008.00715.x

Vogel, S. & Garcia, O. (2017). Translanguaging. In G. Noblit & L. Moll, eds., *Oxford Research Encyclopedia of Education*. Oxford: Oxford University Press.

Walqui, A. (2006). Scaffolding instruction for English language learners: A conceptual framework. *International Journal of Bilingual Education and Bilingualism*, 9, 159–80. doi: 10.1080/13670050608668639

Walqui, A. & van Lier, L. (2010). *Scaffolding the Academic Success of Adolescent English Language Learners: A Pedagogy of Promise*. San Francisco ÇA: WestEd.

Wang, D. (2019). *Multilingualism and Translanguaging in Chinese Language Classroom*. Cham, Denmark: Palgrave Macmillan.

Williams, C. (1994). *Arfarniad o Ddulliau Dysgu ac Addysgu yng Nghyddestun Addysg Uwchradd Ddwyieithog* [An evaluation of teaching and learning methods in the context of bilingual secondary education]. Unpublished doctoral thesis, University of Wales, Bangor. https://research.bangor.ac.uk/portal/files/20574535/null

Williams, C. (1996). Secondary education: Teaching in the bilingual situation. In C. Williams, G. Lewis & C. Baker, eds. *The Language Policy: Taking Stock*. Llangefni, UK: CAI, pp. 39–78.

Williams, C. (2000). Bilingual teaching and language distribution at 16+. *International Journal of Bilingual Education and Bilingualism*, 3, 129–48. doi: 10.1080/13670050008667703

Williams, C. (2002). *A Language Gained: A Study of Language Immersion at 11–16 Years of Age*. Bangor, UK: School of Education. www.bangor.ac.uk/education-and-human-development/publications/Language_Gained%20.pdf

Williams, C. (2003). *Learning in two languages. Dysgu Mewn Dwy Iaith*. Bangor: University of Wales Bangor.

Williams, C. (2012). *The National Immersion Scheme Guidance for Teachers on Subject Language Threshold: Accelerating the Process of Reaching the Threshold*. Bangor, UK:The Welsh Language Board.

Woll, N. (2018). Investigating dimensions of metalinguistic awareness: What think-aloud protocols revealed about the cognitive processes involved in positive transfer from L2 to L3. *Language Awareness*, 27, 167–85. doi: 10.1080/09658416.2018.1432057

Wood, D., Bruner, J. S. & Ross, G. (1976). The role of tutoring in problem solving. *Journal of Child Psychology, Psychiatry, & Applied Disciplines*, 17, 89–100.

Acknowledgements

This work was supported by the Spanish Ministry of Science and Innovation [Grant Number FEDERPID2019-105818GB-100] and the Basque Government [Grant Number DREAM IT-1225-19].

Elements in Language Teaching

Heath Rose

Linacre College, University of Oxford

Heath Rose is an Associate Professor of Applied Linguistics at the University of Oxford. At Oxford, he is course director of the MSc in Applied Linguistics for Language Teaching. Before moving into academia, Heath worked as a language teacher in Australia and Japan in both school and university contexts. He is author of numerous books, such as Introducing Global Englishes, The Japanese Writing System, Data Collection Research Methods in Applied Linguistics, and Global Englishes for Language Teaching. Heath's research interests are firmly situated within the field of second language teaching, and include work on Global Englishes, teaching English as an international language, and English Medium Instruction.

Jim McKinley

University College London

Jim McKinley is an Associate Professor of Applied Linguistics and TESOL at UCL, Institute of Education, where he serves as Academic Head of Learning and Teaching. His major research areas are second language writing in global contexts, the internationalisation of higher education, and the relationship between teaching and research. Jim has edited or authored numerous books including the Routledge Handbook of Research Methods in Applied Linguistics, Data Collection Research Methods in Applied Linguistics, and Doing Research in Applied Linguistics. He is also an editor of the journal, System. Before moving into academia, Jim taught in a range of diverse contexts including the US, Australia, Japan and Uganda.

Advisory Board

About the Series

This Elements series aims to close the gap between researchers and practitioners by allying research with language teaching practices, in its exploration of research-informed teaching, and teaching-informed research. The series builds upon a rich history of pedagogical research in its exploration of new insights within the field of language teaching.

Cambridge Elements ᵔ

Elements in Language Teaching

Elements in the Series